Seven Steps to an Award-Winning School Library Program

7 Steps
to an
Award-Winning
School Library
Program

Ann M. Martin

Foreword by Ruth Toor

LIBRARIES
U N L I M I T E D
A Member of the Greenwood Publishing Group

Westport, Connecticut ● London

Library of Congress Cataloging-in-Publication Data

Martin, Ann M.
    Seven steps to an award-winning school library program / by Ann M. Martin
      p. cm.
    Includes index.
    ISBN 1-59158-173-7
    1. School libraries--United States. 2. Instructional materials centers--United States. 3.
Media programs (Education)--United States. I. Title.
Z675.S3M2734   2005
027.8--dc22   2005047485

British Library Cataloguing in Publication Data is available.

Library of Congress Catalog Card Number: 2005047485
ISBN: 1–59158–173–7

First published in 2005

Libraries Unlimited, 88 Post Road West, Westport, CT 06881
A Member of the Greenwood Publishing Group, Inc.
www.lu.com

Printed in the United States of America

The paper used in this book complies with the
Permanent Paper Standard issued by the National
Information Standards Organization (Z39.48–1984).

10 9 8 7 6 5 4 3 2 1

May this book serve as a living legacy to my family, my friends, and my colleagues whose affirmation of my vision served as the inspiration and encouragement for this book.

Contents

Foreword

Everyone dreams of having an award-winning media center with an exemplary program admired by faculty, administrators, students, and parents. Although reviewing and carrying out the precepts of *Information Power* can help bring your media center to its highest potential, what you really need is a living model demonstrating and helping you understand the ways its principles have been incorporated. Ann Martin gives you this opportunity in this book, written in response to questions about how to qualify for the National School Library Media Program of the Year (NSLMPY) Award.

As a member of the NSLMPY selection committee, I first met Ann when we visited the James River High School Library. Reading her description of its program, which brought back wonderful memories to me of the "friendly, welcoming environment" of that exciting place, should help and inspire those of you trying to emulate her success as you see the many creative ways media specialists and teachers work together to benefit their students.

Throughout her eight chapters, the author holds your hand, helping you with the detailed steps of preparing your media center and then the NSLMPY application documenting what you have done. She offers good advice on working with teachers and suggestions for leadership, ranging from 15-minute "Rapid Fire" research instruction, to "Lunch in the Library" presentations, to "tailor-made lessons designed by library media specialists in collaboration with the teacher." Her yearlong reading project, GO READ, allows students and the school community to "grow and be enriched," fomenting excitement and learning in a different way.

These units (with helpful summaries at the end) explain first how to "align your program with *Information Power* . . . providing a framework where the reader uses national standards to meet local user needs," then describe how to build effective teams; conduct an evaluation of your current program through various methods, hearing (and following) the message presented; create goals "as needs are identified"; address teacher resistance to change; ensure that the library program is fully integrated into the curriculum; deliver different training methods during school time, working in groups to help solve problems; and relate to your core users through a novel advocacy plan. All this leads up to the final chapter—applying for the award itself—which sets forth a time line for the 10-step sequence that takes about three months to complete, as well as a strategy for the NSLMPY Committee's site visit.

In addition, the appendixes, including joint planning and evaluation forms, statements of goals and objectives, surveys, sample lesson plans, and workshop plans and materials, offer new ideas for ways to expand your activities. As Ann Martin concludes, whether or not you win the NSLMPY, it is definitely worth the doing, because your program will have changed for the better.

Ruth Toor
January 2005

Acknowledgments

I am deeply grateful to the many administrators, teachers, students, and librarians who share the vision of an active *Information Power*–driven library media program. Their willingness to pursue change and increase student achievement provided the background and evidence that guided the framework for this book.

I would like to thank and acknowledge the following individuals for their assistance with this book.

- The staff and students of James River High School, who lived the tenets of this book.

- Susanne Kelly, who reviewed the work as it developed and gave invaluable comments and suggestions.

- Sarah J. Susbury, who introduced me to the work of Michael Fullan, and provided graphic assistance and technical support.

- Ruth Toor, who graciously provided the foreword for this book.

- ALA, who gave permission to quote and reprint essential information.

- Sharon Coatney, acquisitions editor, Libraries Unlimited, for her thoughtful editorial guidance and assistance.

Finally, I am deeply grateful to my husband Charlie Martin and my children, Beth Fisher and Andy Martin, and their families. They gave me the encouragement, understanding, and precious time needed to research and write this book.

Introduction

To facilitate national implementation of the principles, standards, philosophy, and vision contained in *Information Power,* the American Association of School Libraries (AASL) sponsors the National School Library Media Program of the Year Award (NSLMPY). "This awards program recognizes that the mission of the school library media program is to ensure that students and staff are effective users of information" (AASL 2004b). Since I received the NSLMPY Award in 2002, many library media specialists and administrators have asked me to examine and explain how a school qualifies to be called the number one school library media program in the country. This book is my answer to those requests. It explains the steps that come before the application process, because applying for the NSLMPY Award is the culmination of aligning a school library media program with *Information Power.* This book also provides tips on how to make the NSLMPY Awards application process efficient and effective.

Information Power details the components of an award-winning library program. *A Planning Guide for Information Power: Building Partnerships for Learning with School Library Media Program Assessment Rubric for the 21st Century* guides advocates for school library program change "through the planning process central to program development and implementation" (AASL 1999, n.p.). The work of Gary Hartzell (2003), David Loertscher, Keith Curry Lance (Lance and Loertscher 2002), and others provides the underpinnings for the implementation of national standards. One might then ask, "Why are so many schools struggling to implement the change necessary to produce an exemplary library program such as one that qualifies for the NSLMPY Award given by the AASL?" Fullan argues that, "Even if you knew how particular schools became collaborative, you could never tell precisely how you should go about it in your own school. There is no magic bullet; research can give us promising lines of thinking but never a complete answer. To some extent, each group must build its own model and develop local ownership through its own process" (2001, n.p.). *Seven Steps to an Award-Winning School Library Program* provides detailed processes that, when combined with local ownership, create a unique, exemplary school library media program.

Translating the principles of *Information Power* into practices that create the ideal library program is not an easy task. The goal of this book is to provide a practical game plan for transforming the mandates of *Information Power* into an exemplary and award-winning school library program. The aim is to provide a framework in which the reader uses the national standards to meet local user needs.

This book describes processes to initiate and implement change, including how to assemble and organize teams, evaluate the current library media program, analyze the evaluation results, identify and overcome barriers to change, develop training models, and create implementation tools. In addition, the book provides a method to create instructional connections. While a school library media program's primary focus must be instruction and increased student achievement, especially in this era of accountability, a key ingredient in creating lifelong users is to develop parallel activities that extend beyond instruction and contribute to a friendly and welcoming environment. Special presentations and programs offered within a library program provide another venue for integration and collaboration with curriculum areas.

Following the seven steps detailed in this book will result in an improved program focused on change, driven by user needs, and guided by program best practices. This book is designed for the building-level library media specialist and for district supervisors wishing to align individual libraries with *Information Power*. Instructors of courses addressing the administration of school library media programs will find this a useful guide for their classes. School administrators will find the seven steps helpful when reviewing their own library programs. The steps needed to achieve authentic library program improvements are detailed for anyone who can initiate and lead the change process.

For library media specialists to move from theory to practical application, the indispensable tools (missing from the literature) are the improvement processes and the training models. Improvement processes and training models are unique inclusions in *Seven Steps to an Award-Winning School Library Program*. These process designs and training principles institutionalize the concepts provided in *Information Power*. This book provides the missing piece necessary to produce an exemplary and award-winning library program.

The challenges of redesigning or rebuilding a library program are great, even overwhelming at times, but from my own experience, the results far outweigh the investments. I hope my book serves as a guide through the process. I commend and encourage you in your efforts and willingness to make positive change in your library program a reality. Best of luck in all of your professional endeavors.

References

American Association of School Librarians (AASL). 1999. *A planning guide for Information Power: Building partnerships for learning with school library media program assessment rubric for the 21st century.* Chicago: American Association of School Librarians/American Library Association.

American Association of School Librarians (AASL). 2004a. *AASL publications and journals: Information Power books & products.* Available at: http://www.ala.org/ala/aasl/aaslpubsandjournals/ informationpowerbook/informationpowerbooks.htm (accessed November 21, 2004).

————. 2004b. *National School Library Media Program of the Year award application.* Chicago. Available at: http://www.ala.org/ ala/aasl/aaslawards/natlslmprogram/2005nslmpyapp.pdf (accessed November 14, 2004).

Fullan, Michael. 2001. *The new meaning of educational change.* 3rd ed. New York: Teachers College Press.

Hartzell, Gary. 2003. *Building influence for the school librarian: Tenets, targets, & tactics.* 2nd ed. Worthington, OH: Linworth Publishing.

Lance, Keith Curry, and David V. Loertscher. 2002. *Powering achievement: School library media programs make a difference: The evidence mounts.* 2nd ed. San Jose, CA: Hi Willow Research & Publishing.

Snapshot of an Award-Winning Library

Introduction

The American Association of School Librarians (AASL), a division of the American Library Association (ALA), is a professional organization for school library media specialists. In 1998 the AASL leadership combined with the leadership of Association for Educational Communications and Technology (AECT) and completed an update to the 1988 edition of *Information Power,* a guidebook for school library media specialists. This guidebook contains a set of nine information literacy standards that encourage best practices for creating an effective library media program. These practices are based on collaboration, technology, and leadership. *Information Power* charges the school library media specialist with the responsibility to provide active learning through teaching information literacy skills in a content-rich environment. The school community benefits by accessing information delivered by a program administered to produce lifelong library users who are skilled to perform in an information-driven society.

To facilitate national implementation of the principles, standards, philosophy, and vision contained in *Information Power,* AASL sponsors the National School Library Media Program of the Year Award (NSLMPY). "This awards program recognizes that the mission of the school library media program is to ensure that students and staff are effective users of information" (AASL 2004). The award's purpose is to

- "[e]mphasize the importance of the school library media program as an integral part of the instructional process, vital to the curriculum for quality education" (AASL 2004);

- "[d]emonstrate the fundamental value of excellent school library media programs in the personal and social development of future leaders, our youth" (AASL 2004);

1

- "[r]ecognize that a variety of models exist for the successful school library media program, and identify positive role models which, through their approaches, may be unique to the specific school community, still share the common goal and principles of meeting the information needs of users" (AASL 2004); and

- "[e]ncourage the development of library media programs that are the result of the collaborative efforts of all those who are responsible for student learning" (AASL 2004).

The Prototype

The school library that achieves the status of the American Association of School Librarian's National School Library Media Program of the Year (NSLMPY) exemplifies the principles of *Information Power*. This award recognizes the school library media program that embodies the principles of *Information Power* and serves as a model for all school library media programs. Claims that these principles are fully actualized within the school community must be documented. It is necessary to benchmark the data and show continuous improvement to give credence to statements indicating the library program is exemplary. Deciding to apply for this award brings validation to the library media specialists and to the library program. Is the effort worth it? Is it even possible to be named number one in the school library field when so many school library programs apply? The answer to both these questions is an unequivocal "yes." Go for the award!

This chapter provides a snapshot of the NSLMPY 2002 award recipient, James River High School, in Chesterfield, Virginia. The subsequent chapters spell out the process to follow when applying for the NSLMPY award. An award-winning program ensures that the library mission statement meets local and district needs and that the library goals and objectives are tied to the mission of the school. Evidence of the library program's alignment with the standards in *Information Power* must be documented. An award-winning library media program is one that is evaluated prior to applying for the NSLMPY award. The evaluation is based on the rubric provided by AASL in *A Planning Guide for Information Power: Building Partnerships for Learning* (AASL 1999). In this guide each target indicator is chronicled with supporting data. Then, areas for growth are identified and new ideas to initiate change are recorded. The James River High School library media specialists used this guide to evaluate the library media program. This chapter provides a snapshot of the James River High School library media program. It includes solid practices and gives viable ideas to replicate even if you do not wish to apply for the NSLMPY award.

The Snapshot

On any given day, the James River High School library is a busy place because students and staff are comfortable and enjoy spending time there. Students encourage their friends to meet them in the library for academic, cultural, and social reasons. Using the expertise of the library media specialists, teachers correlate subject area curriculum with library resources. Every library moment reflects the James River library mission to meet the lifelong learning needs of the students and staff through a teaching partnership that integrates information literacy with each curriculum area's standards of learning. The library media program supports this mission by serving as the focal point of the information network within and outside the walls of the school. Library goals and objectives target activities that develop lifelong learners, encourage love of literature, and promote independent seekers of information. *Information Power* is the keystone of the library program.

Candid comments about the library program from stakeholders in the school indicate that the library is vibrant. All segments of the school community value the library media center and express support of the library media specialists and the principles of *Information Power:*

- "Our students are most fortunate to have you as professionals who support curricular innovations and make high school come alive! Thanks for all that you do to make this school special."—John Titus, JRHS principal

- "Their willingness to break new ground instructionally, their support of teachers and curriculum above and beyond what is expected, and their professional attitude make working with them such a pleasure."—Tim Couillard, JRHS physics teacher

- "This epitomizes what a library should be—a place for knowledge, contemplation, and growth. James River High School is fortunate to have a library that does not merely pay lip service to these ideas, but actively works to incorporate them into our school community." —Laura Lay, JRHS Social Studies Department chair

- "The librarians have expressed a keen interest in my work and asked for a copy of my novel, *Fortune's Ruin*, to circulate through the library. It felt great to have people interested in what I worked hard to accomplish, and this boosted my confidence in writing."—Evan Thomas Moore, JRHS student 2003

The three categories of *Information Power*—learning and teaching, information access and delivery, and program administration—plus the public relations efforts that advocate the entire program, frame this snapshot of the James River High library program. For that reason, this award-winning program description is organized under the major components described in *Information Power*.

Learning and Teaching

This section explains how the James River library media specialists encourage reading, research, and assessment. It also explains how teaching information literacy standards, creating effective scheduling, and partnering for collaboration encourage students and staff to be effective users of information. The principles for learning and teaching from *Information Power* are found in appendix A.

Daily instruction is based on the principles outlined in the national standards found in appendix A. Every student, regardless of curriculum tract or intellectual level, receives information literacy skills. From the mildly mentally disabled (MIMD) program, to the guitar program, to the technical drawing program, to the English as a Second Language (ESL) program, to the core curriculum subjects, students are brought to the library media center for projects and reading assignments. The different programs within the school are strengthened through library connections. In addition to working with students across the standard disciplines, the library media specialists meet with every ESL student, every MIMD student, and every student enrolled in the Leadership and International Relations Specialty School. Targeted materials for each of these curriculum areas are ordered. The library media specialists publicize these distinct resources to the teachers of the individual programs. By reaching out to special programs, the library media specialists expand the library to all segments of the school community.

An open-door policy for staff allows them access to the library before, during, and after school for both planning and collaboration. Throughout the day students arrive individually and in small groups, with requests ranging from assistance in opening a computer file brought from home to stock market analysis to PowerPoint™ presentations. Search strategy sheets (see appendix B) are provided to students as a research organizational tool. The form assists students in developing individual research plans by providing space to list the topic to investigate, keywords, related topics, and possible sources of information.

The library media specialists focus skills instruction on accessing, synthesizing, evaluating, and using information. Teaching library media specialists, who serve as instructional partners in the educational process, facilitate the integration of information literacy with the curriculum area standards of learning. The James River High School library joint planning form (see appendix B) assists this collaboration by requesting that the teacher indicate research needs prior to the class library visit. The information from the planning form serves as the basis for an information literacy lesson plan. As a result, each class receives a tailor-made lesson designed by one of the library media specialists in collaboration with the teacher. Students are then instructed on information literacy skills through a variety of teaching methods that address the diverse learning styles of the students. Reinforcement of the skills is immediate as students do research in a lablike setting with a wide range of resources.

Library media specialists believe that information is power and that resources extend beyond the walls of the building. Information is available through electronic databases, print, and Internet resources at school and at home. Varied levels of print and electronic resources meet student needs. Evaluation of each library experience is accomplished through direct observation, student discussion, project evaluation, and rubrics. Since there is no one formula for finding information, the library media specialists encourage students to explore and share their research strategies and results. All players in the research process benefit from the students' analysis of their research experience. The evaluative information on the availability of resources assists in prioritizing future acquisitions.

Research projects developed by the teachers combine with library information literacy lessons to target individual and collaborative inquiry. The library program accommodates all levels of research, from fact finding to in-depth explorations. Part of the joint planning form lists curriculum standards of learning and information literacy standards to show how they interweave to best meet student information goals. Copies of the joint planning form and lesson plan (see appendix B) are provided to the teacher and administrators prior to the class visit.

Collaboration precipitates instructional brainstorming between teachers and the library media specialist. This cooperation results in novel and diverse teaching strategies that focus on information literacy skills and inquiry-based learning. Book chats, open forums, and guest speakers combine with traditional teaching tools to provide students with cognitive and intrinsic learning that results in lifelong information skills.

The library program "encourages and engages students in reading, viewing, and listening for understanding and enjoyment" (ALA and AECT 1998, 66). A wide range of information and recreational reading sources for scholastic and personal needs, as well as comfortable seating, encourage these pursuits. An example of one literacy outreach is a community reading project. In this yearlong reading project the entire school membership reads a selected book. The teachers and library media specialists coordinate activities that tie the book selection to the curriculum. Each of the nearly

2,000 students and more than 150 staff members, including clerical, custodial, and cafeteria workers in the school, receives his or her own copy of the book to read. The superintendent provides funding because the program is unique and helps students individually, and the school community collectively, grow and be enriched (Titus 2002). This reading project expanded into the community and is known in the metro area as GO READ.

An outcome of GO READ is a closer working relationship among schools, public libraries, and businesses in the greater metro area. The school libraries are the focal point for launching the community read within the metro area (Figure 1.1).

Figure 1.1. Students kick off the community GO READ program with 30 minutes' sustained silent reading.

The community finances an author visit, and students attend a question-and-answer session with the author. Besides the privilege of students meeting a living author, the greatest benefit of this program is that students are able to discuss tough issues in a safe environment. The library media specialists, the principal, and the superintendent championed intellectual freedom when naysayers attempted to stop the project in the schools. Activities such as book chats and open forums allow students to discuss the book's themes and internalize the message. Teachers, parents, administrators, and students work together to promote literacy. Student-run clubs visit elementary schools to read companion books to younger students. These companion books convey the theme expressed in the high school selection and provide an opportunity for family members to sit around the table and discuss relevant issues.

Information Access and Delivery

Part of the framework of an effective library media program is how information is accessed and delivered to its users. The standards that measure the effectiveness of a school library media program with regard to information access and delivery refer to the physical facility, the materials available, and the scheduling of the library media center. In addition, effective information access and delivery ensures intellectual freedom and the ethical use of information. The principles for information access and delivery from *Information Power* are found in appendix A. This section shows how the award-winning program at James River met the goals of information access and delivery.

An important part of the James River High School library media program's mission is open access to the library media center, unlimited access to information, and extension of the library resources to the school community. Guided by district policies on the selection and development of collections, the James River High School library media specialists seek input from staff and students in the resource development process. The library media specialists provide bibliographic assistance to teachers for their curriculum areas that includes print, electronic resources, and Internet sites.

The physical layout of the library allows for multiple classes as well as small groups. A closed computer lab and a conference room allow for quiet, reflective work, and comfortable seating is available for students to gather and relax. The entire collection is available for overnight checkout, and teachers often continue lessons in their classrooms using library materials. Library resources are networked throughout the school and the district. When needs arise, the library media specialists reach out to the larger community, including public, university, research, and corporate libraries, for specialized resources.

Students and staff are encouraged to use library resources at a time that is most convenient for them, including extended hours and lunch periods. A need expressed in parent and student surveys prompted the library media specialists to extend the library's hours of operation until 6:00 P.M. every Wednesday. Teachers plan due dates for assignments on Thursday or Friday and promote using these extended hours. Electronic databases and an online public access catalog (OPAC) provide home access 24 hours, seven days a week.

Library media specialists support the concept of intellectual freedom and seek support through the district selection policy. Challenges to the community-wide reading project were effectively addressed by school administration and central office staff. The district director of technology requested the head librarian's participation in examining intellectual freedom issues surrounding filtering, selection, and challenges.

Students are aware of and sign acceptable use policy and computer code of ethics forms (see appendix B). The school and district have developed written policies on information selection and challenged materials, and the library media specialists use these tools when necessary. In the teaching/learning process, the librarians' objectives for each lesson include documentation of resources, respect for the ownership of ideas, and the ethics surrounding the utilization of information resources. The James River library media specialists, in conjunction with the English Department, developed and adopted a uniform electronic bibliographic format for use throughout the school.

Program Administration

Managing the library media center effectively depends on appropriate staffing, management procedures, planning, program funding, staff development, and program assessment. The principles for program administration from *Information Power* are found in appendix A. Program administration frames the third element of an award-winning library media program. The following description illustrates the components of a well-managed library media program.

The James River High School library media staff recognize that "a well-run, student-centered school library media program that is carefully planned, appropriately staffed, and imaginatively and efficiently managed is essential for meeting contemporary learning needs" (ALA and AECT 1998, 101). The library media specialists report directly to the principal because of his interest in and support for the library media program. This results in effective two-way communication with administration concerning library needs and leads to support in scheduling, funding, and intellectual freedom issues. The principal recognizes the administrative demands of the library and does not encumber library media specialists' time with duty periods or tasks that pull them from the library. As an advocate of the library media program in the community, the principal raises the library's visibility to the public by promoting the program as a key component of student academic success. The head librarian is a member of the Principal's Advisory Committee (PAC), which consists of department heads and meets bimonthly.

One way to meet the changing needs of users is to conduct ongoing evaluation of the library program. For this reason a needs analysis of staff and students is performed periodically to assess the library media program. Goals and objectives (see appendix B) developed as a result of the needs analysis are reviewed by the library media specialists and updated annually, based on changing curriculum, technology, and user needs. These goals are listed under each of the three major information literacy areas: teaching and learning, information access and delivery, and program administration. Every October the principal reviews the goals.

Collection development is ongoing based on input from teachers and students as well as from reviews. The library media specialists weed and update the collection on a systematic cycle to provide accurate, current information in all the Dewey resource sections. Observation of student research assists the librarians in identifying student information needs.

The librarians stay current on library issues through membership in professional organizations and through reading professional journals. They make attendance at regional, state, and national conferences a priority and are active participants on action committees and presenters at conferences advocating for school library programs. When difficult library concerns arise, the library media specialists rely on the expertise and advice available to them through their colleagues and the leadership in these professional organizations.

Accounting guidelines provided by the district are strictly adhered to for county and local funds. An annual report detailing resources and expenditures is filed with the school and the county. When there is a need for additional funds, the library media specialists apply for awards and grants. On one occasion the library media specialists administered a technology fund drive to update the library computers. Budget allocations are stretched whenever possible. A district acquisitions department provides group discounts for materials. Teacher support for full funding of the library budget is a direct result of effective communication between the library media specialists and the individual teachers.

During all open house programs, parents and students are invited to preview the library resources. The library media specialists offer home access database training sessions to parents. Effective training comes from the top down; thus the library media specialists train administrators and department chairs first and then the teachers in the departments, using the department chair as part of the training team. Ongoing one-on-one training is conducted on an as-needed basis.

At the building level, the library program is promoted through monthly articles in the school newsletter, the student newspaper, and monthly reports; at all PTSA meetings, PAC meetings, and open houses; and by visits from people from other school districts. The librarians encourage communication within the feeder school pattern and initiate meetings with the middle school librarians and their principals. They attend formal and informal meetings with other high school librarians to share tips and ideas.

District policy and procedures help in the management of the library media program. At the building level, processes have been developed to ensure equitable, efficient, timely, and easy access to resources. Such tools as scheduling calendars, joint planning forms, search strategy sheets, e-mail, student aide assessment forms, PowerPoint presentations, and tip sheets on software applications and bibliographic format assist in the efficient management of the library.

The greatest asset in the James River High School program is the library staff, who work as a team to seamlessly connect users with resources. This is accomplished because each member is cross-trained and willingly steps in for others throughout the day to ensure uninterrupted service for library users. Because library staff have a common work ethic and a sense of urgency to fulfill the diverse requests of students and staff, the school library is an effective, efficient, well-run program.

Public Relations

The library program's public relations initiative is clearly framed by *Information Power*. A public relations effort with *Information Power* as the foundation boosts the library program while reaching out to its users and makes the public aware of the school library media program and its potential. The library media specialists use each of the different principles in *Information Power* to reach out to the school community. For example, under the principle "Learning and Teaching," the program exemplifies principles 1, 3, 6, 7, 10 (see appendix A). In "Information Access and Delivery," the public relations program highlights principles 3 and 4 (see appendix A). In "Program Administration," principle 9 (clear communication of the mission, goals, functions, and impact of the library media program is necessary to the effectiveness of the program) is well documented in monthly reports, school newsletters, the student newspaper, local television coverage, and communiqués from the principal at PTSA meetings (ALA and AECT 1998, 100).

The high level of acceptance of teacher collaboration and curriculum integration at the James River library validates the importance of the library program in the school. Through targeted instruction of staff on *Information Power*, evaluation of Web sites, and best use of block scheduling, the library media specialists encourage teacher library use. The library media specialists use every opportunity to educate the staff about the new materials that will make their jobs easier, more fun, and creative. At the beginning of the year, a new teacher orientation includes an overview of the library program. When new materials demand new information literacy skills, the library media specialists initiate training sessions to update the teachers on these resources. Training is structured to accommodate the limited time available in a teacher's schedule. The library media specialists also creatively allocate time by suggesting a variety of ways to utilize the library for research. "Rapid Fire" lessons are designed to provide students with brief review activities that use small blocks of time. These lessons encourage teachers to come to the library for 15-minute research opportunities. The students love the variety these "Rapid Fire" lessons give their day, and the teachers expand their classroom walls to teach in a new environment. Instructional connections for every activity, idea, and event that the library media specialists brainstorm use teacher input. This inclusion results in library literacy and curriculum-related programs that teachers and their students endorse and support.

Approachable access to the library is evident as students and teachers meet through a variety of opportunities. Because of the comfortable atmosphere, the library media center is considered a place for collegial fun, where up-to-date information on the latest news at school, in the community, and throughout the world is available. The teachers also view the library as intellectually stimulating, and they come to read the newspaper or share in free-flowing discussions. This means that the library media center is regarded as a safe zone where multiple activities and individuals come together.

Students are essential to the library program's success, and students and their parents are invited into the library often. The library media specialists know that students love recognition. In addition, they realize that high school students' parents love to see their children recognized and to see them perform. Parents are issued invitations to the library whenever their students' work or skills are on display. Following are some of the ways the library media program attracts students and their parents into the library:

- Student displays feature the talents of individuals while advertising curriculum programs in the school (Figure 1.2).

**Figure 1.2. An art display highlights student talent
and illustrates curriculum connections.**

- Sometimes special activities are highlighted in the library display case. Often these displays involve student participation, such as the *Things They Carried* community reading project display (Figure 1.3).

Figure 1.3. Students contribute memorabilia that they carry every day to illustrate the book *The Things They Carried* by Tim O'Brien.

- The library media specialists anticipate student needs for basic supplies such as tape, scissors, a three-hole punch, markers, and disks. They provide these emergency supplies to students who find themselves in a pinch finishing a project.

- The library media specialists even allow students to charge minimal amounts to their accounts when they run short for copies or lunch.

Other members of the school community are made aware of the school library media program and its potential. Administrators, staff, students, parents, central office staff, and school board members enjoy and participate in special programs. One such program is entitled "Lunch in the Library." This is a series of special presentations that connect curriculum to real-life applications and take place in the library during lunch. Principal John Titus (2003) said, "The genius of the program is in its simplicity. These programs encourage curriculum connections, collaboration, real-life application, and community inclusion. Teachers in multiple curriculum areas work together with the library media specialists to present monthly programs. The "Lunch in the Library" presentations validate class work and introduce the community to the school. A sample of some of the programs and their connections follows:

• The "Physics of Magic" program highlighted the principles of physics used by many magicians. This program connected physics to the career magician (Figure 1.4).

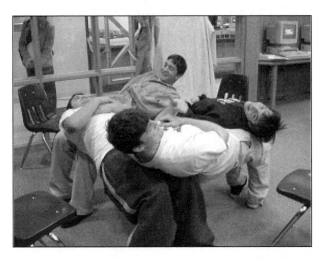

Figure 1.4. Students participate in a magic act in which the principles of physics create an illusion.

• The focus of the "Point Counter Point" program was on the differing views our country held during the Vietnam War. Two social studies teachers debated the issues surrounding the Vietnam War. One provided the social activist's view, while the other vocalized the conservative view. Connections to social studies, debate procedures, and life in the 1960s drew students into the library during lunch for "Point Counter Point" (Figure 1.5).

Figure 1.5. Linda Boggs and Bill Bray, teachers of social studies, share their expertise on the Vietnam War and reenact a debate from the 1960s.

- "Letters from Home," created by the theater classes, consisted of war letters researched by the students and developed into monologues for presentation. This program connected to English and social studies classes.

- Another theater student monologue program entitled "Love Stinks" elicited laughs and tears during a February lunch program (Figure 1.6).

Figure 1.6. Theater students perform "Love Stinks," monologues on love, during the February "Lunch in the Library."

- Another "Lunch in the Library" program was a deep-sea diving presentation that connected a teacher's hobby with the physical education, science, and photography curricula.

- The "Prom Fashion Show" utilized the expertise of marketing students. The marketing students decided on a theme, contacted formal wear companies, designed the stage, provided publicity, decided on background music, and created a written dialog for the show. The presentation used skills that the students were taught while appealing to the high school students' interest in prom fashions (Figure 1.7).

Figure 1.7. Fashion students demonstrate modeling and marketing skills during "Lunch in the Library."

In celebration of reading and literacy, the library media specialists modeled a reading promotion on the celebrity reading posters from ALA. During the first year, students and staff chose their favorite books, and the library media specialists took their pictures with a digital camera, transferred them into PowerPoint, and then printed the pictures and posted them. During the next year students and staff were asked to choose their favorite children's book (Figure 1.8).

Figure 1.8. Amiee Anthony holds her favorite children's book next to a self-portrait she completed. Note the picture of Amiee when she was in grade school. The art teacher's project integrated the art curriculum with the library media specialists' focus on reading "then and now."

When the pictures are removed from the library walls, they are placed in notebooks. These notebooks aid the library media specialists with book selection and title recommendations while encouraging reading as a life-long pleasure. Another way to highlight students with this project is to show the pictures in kiosk fashion through PowerPoint™. Students flock to the library to see themselves and their friends in these PowerPoint kiosk presentations.

Other picture albums on display highlight activities such as home-coming, Halloween, prom, robotics, and graduation. The library media specialists snap pictures or ask for pictures and then place them in albums in the library media center.

An additional activity that is relatively simple to accomplish but expands the walls of the library media center is the SAT question of the day. This is available online through the College Board Web site. Current news displays connect students with events such as the Iraq War, Nobel Prize recipients, and sports results. Through book displays that coincide with these events, reading suggestions connect books and student work to the curriculum.

Another public relations opportunity for outreach is the library media center's holiday social. The outreach for this is extensive and unique because all staff, students, parents, and community gather informally to enjoy a relaxed time together. The library media specialists pull in student service clubs such as the Beta Club, Key Club, and National Honor Society to help with the social. The school's orchestra plays background music that generates a relaxed atmosphere.

The library media specialists sponsor clubs based on their own interests. This is a wonderful public relations tool. In addition, the library media specialists are viewed as a team and compete in contests together. They are all parents and view the students as though they are their own. The specialists attend school events and are active professionally on the local, state, and national levels.

The library media specialists know that the library media program can connect to anything in the school, and students are invited to cover events through the Web site and the school newspaper. The library media specialists feed the student journalists the stories. The school system's public relation's department is provided information about all library-related events.

The staff at James River High School is open to the challenges of innovative ideas. Their major concern is improving student learning. They are willing to connect their curriculum with the library media curriculum because they value improved student achievement. This philosophy, developed through training and teamwork, has won over each staff member one department, one person at a time.

Hopefully, this snapshot of a National School Library Media Program of the Year winner will prove that *any* idea can become an information literacy opportunity, and that it is not necessarily how big or how little the project is but how, where, when, and to whom *Information Power* is connected!

Summary

To be named the National School Library Media Program of the Year means that, based on national standards set forth by the American Association of School Librarians, the school library program is judged the best in the United States that year. More specifically, it means that a comprehensive assessment of the library program by a team of national evaluators has verified that the library program positively affects student achievement. In this day of accountability, this award validates the connection between the library program and the school's instructional needs. Daily library operations based on the standards set forth in *Information Power* are important factors in achieving this award. The library media specialists are evaluated on how well they instruct students in information literacy skills, how well they reinforce these skills, and how well they accommodate all levels of research, from fact finding to in-depth inquiries. Extremely important is how the library media specialists collaborate with teachers to integrate information literacy skills into meaningful results for the students in their individual subject areas. An effective library media program ensures that students are effective users of ideas and information.

References

American Association of School Librarians (AASL). 1999. *A planning guide for Information Power: Building partnerships for learning with school library media program assessment rubric for the 21st century.* Chicago: American Association of School Librarians/American Library Association.

———. 2004. *National School Library Media Program of the Year award application.* Chicago. Available at: http://www.ala.org/ala/aasl/aaslawards/natlslmprogram/2005nslmpyapp.pdf (accessed May 3, 2004).

American Library Association (ALA) and the Association for Educational Communications and Technology (AECT). 1998. *Information power: Building partnerships for learning.* Chicago: American Library Association and the Association for Educational Communications.

Titus, John. 2002. Letter to American Association of School Librarians, January 17.

———. 2003. Letter to American Association of School Librarians, January 28.

Step 1 Creating a Team

As stated in the previous chapter, the school library that achieves the status of AASL's National School Library Media Program of the Year (NSLMPY) exemplifies the principles of *Information Power*. An award-winning library program is the result of planning and organization. The program at James River High School is the outcome of systematic, continuous improvement. The school and the library program grew up together. Prior to its opening in 1994, the principal and department chairs spent months exploring how new technologies could and should be integrated into the curriculum. At these meetings it was evident that although the principal endorsed the full integration of information literacy skills into the curriculum through collaboration with the library media specialist, the department leadership of the school was unaware of the power behind an *Information Power*–driven library. When staff for each department were hired, most teachers were unfamiliar with electronic catalogs, *Information Power*, collaborative teaching, database resources, and library use for all subject areas. The staff viewed the library media center as an additional resource to extend the curriculum for their students. So how can a library media specialist transform a school community's stereotypical perception of a library media program to one in which the principles of *Information Power* are fully actualized? One way is to assemble and organize teams whose charge is to help refine and communicate the vision and mission of the library media program. Once established, these teams guide the library staff through a self-evaluation, a needs analysis, and the adoption of an action plan. Two teams are formed; the first team is composed of the library media staff and the second of members from the school community.

This chapter provides tips to the library media specialist on how to build effective teams or committees. The process includes

- identifying team members,

- explaining team roles,

- defining team tasks,

- developing a time line,

- conducting effective meetings, and

- creating cohesive goals.

Effective teams become the vehicle for small adjustments to or a major overhaul of the library program. Teams validate the connection between the library program and the school's instructional needs by assessing the current program, brainstorming solutions to weaknesses, and implementing new initiatives. Changes that result from teamwork keep the library program vibrant and exciting. When applying for the NSLMPY award, these teams verbalize feedback for the application essays and later for the visiting team.

Identifying Team Members

Educational teams intimidate the most accomplished library media specialist. The idea that someone outside the library department might gain control of the program is frightening. For this reason, the core team concept is recommended so that control and leadership of the project is in the hands of the experts. As the owner of the library program improvement project, the core team provides leadership to the schoolwide team. The library staff makes an effective core team because they *are* the experts in the library field and can manage the project, including setting guidelines for selection of a schoolwide team.

Helpful criteria for selecting members of the larger team include determining whether they are able to

- perceive expectations quickly,

- focus on shared goals,

- share leadership responsibilities,

- resolve problems,

- communicate effectively, and

- meet deadlines.

When deciding whom to include on the schoolwide team, the core team that reviews each potential candidate for these qualities formulates a committee that will get results.

The composition of the schoolwide team should be small rather than large. An ideal team has between seven and ten members and includes the following key people:

- core team members,

- internal stakeholders,

- power brokers, and

- key community members.

Core team members are experts in the field. Depending on the size of the library staff, the head library media specialist and assistant library media specialist might be the only members of the core team on the schoolwide team.

Stakeholders are all those who are affected by the library media program. The internal stakeholders are the staff and students. Two or three teachers should be chosen to represent different curriculum areas or programs in the school. Ideally these teachers already embrace the library program. This *does not* mean that they understand the information literacy standards, but it *does* mean that they use the library personally to meet their needs. Although choosing teachers who are library users is not an absolute requirement, it will make the work more productive and positive. Next, choose two or three students who are representative of the diverse student population. Students will bring an entirely different perspective to the team. They are the largest population the school librarian serves and greatly influence the program's impact.

Power brokers are those school personnel who have political and economic influence. They are usually those who control resources such as time and money. Obviously, an administrator is needed to fill this position. Also consider asking a school board representative to sit on the team.

Brainstorm the names of *key community members* to invite to be on the team. Parents often serve well in this position. Not only are parents interested in what is helpful to their children, but they often can be influential with segments outside of the school walls.

Once the team has been created the members must be prepared to serve as advocates, trainers, and models for the rest of the school community. So choose participants who are interested in the library, honest in assessing needs, and effective in communicating information.

Explaining Team Roles

A basketball coach once said that every member of the team—even those who sit on the bench—has a purpose and role to play. Not only are the bench players the second line for the team, they are necessary for productive team practice. The core team and the schoolwide team are composed of a variety of members from the school community, and each needs to understand his or her role on the team. There are no second string players on this team because each member is a first string player whose goal is to achieve library program change.

The core team's responsibilities include

- serving as content experts,

- providing leadership for the project,

- holding the schoolwide team accountable,

- creating a project time line with deadlines,

- approaching identified candidates to ask if they will participate on the team,

- answering questions concerning the extent of the responsibilities and expected time commitment for each member, and

- communicating the project goal to the schoolwide team.

For each team member to understand the purpose of the work, the core team should have a handout with the preliminary project goals, objectives, and time line available to give each person considering working on the schoolwide team. An example of a schoolwide team fact sheet created specifically for a schoolwide team explaining such a project is in appendix B. Once the candidates agree to serve on the schoolwide team, the core team provides each with background information on *Information Power*. One way to find the most up-to-date articles about *Information Power* is to go to a magazine index database and search under the phrase *Information Power* in quotes. Another option is to visit the AASL Web site and follow links to journals and publications. Also, purchasing the *Information Power: Building Partnerships for Learning* brochure (ISBN 0-8389-8169-0), which lists the nine information literacy standards and suggests ways that *Information Power* can benefit students, teachers, library media specialists, and administrators is helpful (AASL 2004).

The schoolwide team's responsibilities include

- representing the larger school community,

- assisting the library staff in improving the library media program,

- bridging the gap between library program needs and their area of concern, and

- verbalizing the needs of the segment of the community that they represent.

Defining Team Tasks

An example of a schoolwide team fact sheet with guidelines that explain the mandates and the direction for the project to the team is in appendix B. In this case the project's mission is to develop an award-winning library media program. The goal is to provide a program that is exemplary and worthy of the NSLMPY award. The objectives are to create a model library program that (a) meets the needs of its users and (b) is exemplary in all target indicators of *Information Power*. A time line is created that is focused and realistic. The goals, objectives, and time line provide the parameters for the project, thereby giving focus to the task. Well-known child psychologist, Dr. James Dobson discusses the need for establishing boundaries within the home because children "derive security from knowing where the boundaries are and who's available to enforce them" (1992, 59). Likewise, teams also need the security of knowing where the boundaries are and who is available to enforce them. One of Dobson's analogies provides a valid illustration of why guidelines are essential. "Imagine yourself driving a car over the Royal Gorge in Colorado. The bridge is suspended hundreds of feet above the canyon floor, and as a first-time traveler, you are uneasy as you cross. Now suppose there were no guardrails on the side of the bridge; where would you steer the car? Right down the middle of the road! Even though you wouldn't plan to hit the protective rails along the side, you'd feel more secure just knowing they were there" (Dobson 1992, 59). This analogy reveals that rules and guidelines produce more freedom, not less. The core team provides guidelines for the schoolwide team, thus freeing them to focus on the task.

The task of the schoolwide team is to facilitate a merging of the library users' needs with the principles outlined in *Information Power*. The team will assist the library staff in

1. evaluating the status of the current library media program,

2. developing and implementing a needs analysis,

3.   comparing the current library media program to target indicators in *Information Power*,

4.   developing an action plan based on results from the needs analysis and the principles of *Information Power*, and

5.   creating a model library media program.

An important element of the schoolwide team members' task is to synthesize the library information literacy goals as stated in *Information Power's* principles for learning and teaching, information access and delivery, and program administration (see appendix A). The team members also interpret curriculum connections between their area of expertise and the library program. It is their task to focus on how the department curriculum correlates to the library curriculum. This correlation provides avenues for collaboration between the library media specialist and the teaching staff. Team members are leaders who resolve inconsistencies in thought and communicate the library media program's goals and objectives to a representative group of staff members. They also need to remain focused and meet projected deadlines.

Developing a Time Line

Time lines provide a schedule of activities or events, usually in chronological order. This is a representation of what key events must be accomplished at a given point in time. When creating a time line, sometimes it is useful to begin with the date the project must be completed and then go backwards with the key dates. If a final date is not important, just begin with the present and move forward. Allow enough time for activities to be completed without providing so much time that the team loses focus. A sample time line, entitled Schoolwide Team Fact Sheet, is in appendix B. Note that for purposes of this project, the schoolwide team's commitment is about three months. Experience on the length of team terms shows that a longer duration is intimidating. Once the schoolwide team is formed, the members will gladly reconvene for future library projects. These projects might be special events or meetings to facilitate applying for the NSLMPY award.

Effective Team Meetings

Effective meetings require planning and organization. Greater success results when the participants know the purpose and goals of the meeting prior to attending. Start each meeting on time to show that you know the participants' time is valuable. Begin the initial team meeting by validating each team member. This nurturing acknowledges the team members' strengths, curriculum expertise, and understanding of their constituents' attitudes and interests. Provide time at the initial meeting for the team members to get to know each other. A climate of trust and respect is necessary for the team to work collaboratively. Remember that team results are more powerful and significant than individual efforts, so nurturing the team concept is essential.

Next establish *ground rules* for the meetings. Identify the team chair, who will field all questions and concerns. The team chair should follow the agenda but allow discussion to flow. The chair must maintain a focus on the topic by summarizing statements, including all important points. Another way to maintain focus is for the chair to restate the information in a constructive way. Often this permits the group to reflect on the conversation, clarifies the ideas expressed, refocuses on the goal, and generates additional opinions and ideas. Open discussion stimulates creative thinking and problem solving. Once the situation is fully explored, the group leader should suggest ways to resolve the issue based on discussion and ask the group for agreement. This agreement, or consensus, is an opinion or position reached by a group as a whole. It means the entire group is in accord. If a meeting is well organized in advance, a group can make decisions expeditiously, expand information from surveys, and generate effective conclusions. A well-run meeting motivates all participants to get involved and keeps decisions fresh because they sense they are personally affected.

An *agenda* is an essential organizing tool because it provides a quick overview of the issues to be discussed and is an outline for minutes. Agendas allow meetings to move forward when a time frame is placed beside each item on the agenda. Sometimes indicating on the agenda which team member is responsible for reporting or introducing the topic for discussion allows the meeting to move forward smoothly. Distribute agendas several days prior to the meeting. This allows the team members to be prepared for the meeting and also gives them an opportunity to add items to the agenda. The agenda is the tool that provides structure to the meeting and enables the team to move forward productively (see sample agenda in appendix B).

During the meeting someone should *record minutes*. For this type of meeting it is better for the minutes to be brief statements that summarize discussion points, followed by the decided outcomes. A list of homework or assignments with the responsible member is provided. The next meeting date and a list of possible future agenda items should be set up before the meeting ends. Minutes should be sent out to the team for review and revision as soon after the meeting as possible. Minutes serve as a reminder to the team members of accomplishments as well as work assignments to be completed prior to the next meeting (see sample form/team meeting minutes in appendix B).

Cohesive Goals

Directing large groups of people toward a cohesive goal requires passion for and belief in that goal. The opportunity to improve the library media program often creates this passion for the core team. In turn, the core team's passion and beliefs motivate the schoolwide team toward the goal of creating an award-winning library program.

Goals that are clearly stated and over which the team has decision-making authority are achievable. The core team's awareness of how change to the library program affects other curriculum departments' need for funds, time, and resources is critical to creating cohesive goals. For this reason, when attempting to achieve change, the core team should present goals that are nonthreatening and beneficial to the school community, because fierce competition for funds, time, and resources creates resistance. Understanding each department's needs is essential when planning change. A winning situation results when the schoolwide team understands that an award-winning library program will make the school function better and result in positive academic achievement for students. For this reason, the core team must continue to recognize fears that surface during discussions and eliminate them before they become road blocks to improvement. (Refer to step 4 on how to understand and overcome barriers to change.) Cohesive goals are the result of all members of the core and schoolwide teams working through their fears and addressing needs. Cohesive goals create momentum toward expected results based on the anticipated improvements.

The purpose of team goals is to

- organize a team,

- manage the team's time,

- ensure a team focus on targeted achievement,

- provide motivation by organizing the vision into achievable steps, and

- measure progress.

As each goal is completed, individual successes encourage the team to move forward. A critical criterion for success is to make sure that the team knows where they have decision-making authority and what they have control over. For example, if a goal requires money, does the team have the ability to control the budget? Unattainable goals are often the result of trying to implement change when there is no authority to facilitate it.

Team goals for creating an award-winning library program include

1. evaluating the status of the current library media program,

2. developing and implementing a needs analysis,

3. comparing the current library media program to target indicators in *Information Power,*

4. developing an action plan based on results from the needs analysis and the principles of *Information Power,* and

5. implementing the action plan objectives.

The goals are clearly stated and are achievable. The team has decision-making authority over the implementation of these goals. The joint work of the two teams serves as a beginning point for the collaboration that is essential to meet the standards of *Information Power.*

Summary

Building effective teams includes identifying team members, explaining team roles, defining team tasks, creating cohesive goals, and developing a time line. The main benefit of effective teams is that they become the vehicle for either small adjustments to or a major overhaul of the library program. A core team is made up of those members who are the experts in the school library field. The core team or library staff manages the project, including setting guidelines for selection of a schoolwide team. A second, larger team, the schoolwide, team includes core team members, internal stakeholders, power brokers, and key community members. These teams validate the connection between the library program and the school's instructional needs by assessing the current program, brainstorming solutions to weaknesses, and implementing initiatives. The core team is responsible for formulating the project's mission, goals, objectives, and time line. The role of the schoolwide team is to represent the larger school community and bridge the gap between the library program needs and their area of concern. The task of the schoolwide team is to facilitate a merging of the library users' needs with the principles outlined in *Information Power.* This is accomplished through well-organized meetings led by the library media specialist. Effective meetings are guided by cohesive goals, a project time line, meeting agendas, and meeting minutes. Changes that result from teamwork keep the library program vibrant and exciting. When applying for the NSLMPY award, these teams verbalize feedback for the application essays and later to the visiting team.

References

American Association of School Librarians (AASL). 2004. *AASL publications and journals: Information Power books & products.* Available at: http://www.ala.org/ala/aasl/aaslpubsandjournals/ informationpowerbook/informationpowerbooks.htm (accessed July 5, 2004).

Dobson, James. 1992. *The new dare to discipline.* Wheaton, IL: Tyndale House Publishers.

Step 2 Getting Started

Now that the core team and schoolwide team are in place, go to the AASL Web site and print a copy of the NSLMPY award application. When reading the requirements for the essays, it becomes clear that the library media specialist must know how to verify that the program is exemplary. To accomplish this, it is critical that the school community understand and believe in the *Information Power* library. A fully actualized library program is the result of the meshing of user needs with the principles of *Information Power*. The purpose of this chapter is to provide the library media specialist with a process that fuses the library staff's vision and mission with the needs of its users. This fusion of user needs with the library media program's components of learning and teaching, information access and delivery, and program administration provides the basis for an action plan that results in an exemplary library media program.

Evaluations provide feedback on what is important to the library staff and its users. One of the greatest fears about conducting an evaluation is that the resulting data will prompt suggestions that are contrary to best practices for the library program. The library media specialist should take the leap and ask for input, no matter how threatening it might appear. Once an idea, concern, or comment surfaces, the ensuing action will be either positive or negative for the library media program. The way in which the library media program benefits from the evaluation is directly related to how effective the library media specialist is in addressing each concern. The concerns are honest views of what is perceived and should not be taken personally. For example, if a comment is made that indicates there are never any library media specialists available at the beginning of the school day, examine why a teacher might say this. If it is because the library media specialist is pulled to assist with hall duty, bus duty, or audiovisual equipment needs, then use this information to make improvements to the morning routine. Negative issues need to be addressed by analyzing what process is broken or what process does not exist to communicate the library point of view to the user. This occurs best in a relaxed atmosphere. For this reason, when receiving suggestions from the schoolwide team members, experience shows that initial acceptance of the idea without evaluating it is beneficial. The way to handle the recommendation is to thank the person who made the suggestion while writing the idea down. Let the person know that all recommendations and concerns will be addressed later in the process. Later, after reviewing the suggestions within the context of *Information Power*, the library media specialist resurfaces the idea in a modified form. Before working with the schoolwide team, it is critical for the library staff to evaluate the library media program and have a clear picture of the library program's needs. Peter Senge (1992) explains that shared vision comes from personal visions. Identifying the personal vision of each library staff member creates a shared vision for the library media program. Initiating change requires that the library staff know where they are and where they want to end up. The library team that is unified on the vision, mission, and goals of the library media program creates a baseline for effective change.

Evaluating the Current Program

Library media specialists who conduct a self-evaluation of their program will become knowledgeable about their library media program's current strengths and weaknesses. Honesty when observing all characteristics of the library media program is the most important requirement of a self-evaluation. Since clear information literacy objectives and goals are essential to the library program, it is important that the library media specialist start the evaluation with the library department. This prevents curriculum area demands and other educational demands from manipulating the library program and shifting the focus away from information literacy. Just as teachers know the curricula for their grade level, select instructional materials, and develop the teaching methods to implement instruction, library media specialists are proficient in their department. Knowing this, a library media specialist must be the driver who advances the library program to its destination of achieving information literacy goals and objectives.

For the library department to develop a plan it is critical that the most important activities and goals be analyzed and perfected. The following process is effective in determining what matters most to the library staff and library users. The individuals from the core team examine their personal vision, mission, and goals for the program. The results from the core team evaluation provide the basis for questions that assess the schoolwide team's satisfaction with the current library media program. Input and suggestions from the schoolwide committee assist in the development of a questionnaire to send out to the school staff. This questionnaire assesses the effectiveness of the library media program as it is perceived by the school staff.

Self-Evaluation Step by Step

The library media department should begin the process by looking at the program as it exists. Each member of the department must understand and believe in the principles outlined in *Information Power: Building Partnerships for Learning*.

1. The library staff starts by reading the vision and mission that currently guide the library program goals and objectives.

2. Each library staff member then lists his or her thoughts about what portion of the library program is most important. The library staff might create the following list:

    • Integration of library skills into the curriculum

    • Flexible scheduling for library use

    • Resources that are current and user-friendly

    • Meeting the needs of users in a timely manner

3. After comparing the lists to the embedded criteria in the vision and mission, ask the question, "Is what the library staff deems important aligned with the vision and mission?"

4. The library staff then analyzes the consistencies and the inconsistencies between what is perceived and what the vision and mission state.

Next the schoolwide team will continue the self-evaluation process by mirroring the library staff's evaluation process.

1. The schoolwide committee and the team develop a list of what they appreciate most about the library program. Asking this question allows the library media specialist to determine whether the library department's priorities and the school community's priorities agree.

2. If the perceptions are in line with the library vision and mission, a preliminary questionnaire is created by the library staff.

3. This questionnaire is handed out to the schoolwide team to answer. The schoolwide team is also asked to refine and clarify the questionnaire (see appendix B for a library media program survey).

4. The final questionnaire is then sent to all staff members.

The results of this survey provide valuable information to library staff about perceptions of the library media program. Then a needs analysis becomes another part of the evaluation process as the core team, with assistance from the schoolwide team, performs a needs analysis. Using data from the needs analysis and the program self-evaluation, the core team and the schoolwide team can create an action plan.

Vision

Data from the staff questionnaire provide the teachers with a view of the library program. A starting point for the schoolwide team is to review the vision and mission in light of the questionnaire results. In AASL's *A Planning Guide for Information Power: Building Partnerships for Learning with School Library Media Program Assessment Rubric for the 21st Century* (1999), a vision is described as a philosophy: "as you work each day in your library media center, you are, consciously or unconsciously, carrying out your vision or philosophy" (AASL 1999, 2).

A program without a vision is filled with distortion. Vision is when, through the power of imagination, the library media specialist dreams of the ideal library media program. The written vision statement is a manifestation of the best the library program can be for that particular school. Clearly defined vision statements are powerful communication tools that provide the library staff and the school with a picture of the future of the library program. Vision statements may be creative but should be realistic and present ideas on how the library program is integrated into the learning community. *In creating a vision, decide what you want the library program to be known for and then define how the program will accomplish this goal.* For example, the following vision statement provides answers about the direction of the library program:

> The library serves as the heart of the school, pumping knowledge through all areas of school life. It fuses information with real life experiences. This is accomplished through resource sharing, research instruction, reading opportunities, and cultural connections. The library is a welcoming place where users explore and discuss intellectual and social issues. A dynamic library program promotes academic achievement and energizes students and staff. *The library program goal is to be a model for other school library programs.*

Consider the vision in terms of *if* and *then:*

- *if* the library serves as the heart of the school, pumping knowledge through all areas of school life;

- *if* it fuses information with real-life experiences;

- *if* this is accomplished through resource sharing, research instruction, reading opportunities, and cultural connections;

- *if* the library is a welcoming place where its users explore and discuss intellectual and social issues; and

- *if* a dynamic library program promotes academic achievement and energizes students and staff—

- *then the library program will be a model for other school library programs.*

The NSLMPY award is only one indication that the library program is reaching the vision's goal.

Mission

The library media specialist and the library team who agree upon a shared vision or philosophy are then prepared to construct a mission *or* to review the current program mission to make sure that the vision and mission are in agreement.

The library media program mission contains the vision of the organization. Chapter 1 of *Information Power* states that "the mission of the library media program is to ensure that students and staff are effective users of ideas and information" (1998, 6). This clear directive provides each library media program with flexibility in how to carry out the mission as it relates to teaching and learning, information access and delivery, and program administration. A mission is the target that the program is striving to reach. It is important that the library staff be in agreement on the library program's mission before meeting with the schoolwide team. It is also important that the library mission be in agreement with the mission of the school for it to be accepted by the school community without skepticism. Note the three unique mission statements below; each conveys the mission of *Information Power* differently.

- "Our mission is to meet the life-long learning needs of our students and staff through a teaching partnership that integrates information literacy with the curriculum area standards of learning."—James River High School Library, Chesterfield, VA

- "The mission of the Corbett Library Program is to ensure that students and staff are effective users of information and ideas."
—Corbett Elementary School, Tucson, AZ

- "The library media center is the intellectual heart of the educational process and a central source of information. The library media center is a teaching and learning laboratory for the entire educational community and an integral partner with the classroom. The library media center provides equitable intellectual and physical access to ideas and information. The BAA/Fenway library further defines its mission as: Teaching students and staff to effectively access, evaluate, use, and communicate information."—BAA/Fenway Library, Boston, MA

Conducting a Needs Analysis

The next step in the evaluation process is to conduct a needs analysis. The integration of information literacy skills into the daily life of teachers and students is successful when the users' needs are met. The best way to find out what people need is to ask them. Needs analyses are usually accomplished through interviews or by administering attitude surveys and questionnaires like the needs analysis survey in appendix B. The trick to finding out what people really think is whom you ask and how you ask them. Setting a nonthreatening tone produces valid assessments and is critical when seeking information about the program. Invite participation from the stakeholders to involve them in the process and to encourage ownership in the library program. How the questions are asked is important. Since the library program is under review, categorize questions under the three major areas designated in *Information Power*. This will focus attention on the areas important for an award-winning library program and will assist the systematic analysis. When formulating questions, allow the respondents space to write additional comments, whether they are completing an interview or a questionnaire. These additional comments clarify their expressed needs.

When conducting a needs analysis, examine environmental factors that affect the program. This exposes outside issues that might affect the implementation of change to the library media program. Outside issues often involve procedures, policy, management style, or other factors. While it may not be feasible to change some factors, developing new ways of addressing them may help. Often teachers cite "lack of time" as a reason for not collaborating. When a problem is identified, it is up to the library media staff to devise a solution. If the teachers express a need for more time, then develop a tool that will expedite the process of collaboration (refer to step 4).

Another important practice when performing a needs analysis is to acknowledge the respondents' expertise in their curriculum areas and express appreciation for their participation in the needs analysis. Writing brief sentences on the survey accomplishes this. Statements such as the following take little space yet convey appreciation: "Thank you for taking the time to complete this evaluation. The library media specialist values your input to assist in improving the library media program."

Whether the needs analysis is face-to-face or indirect, pay close attention to what is being expressed. Hearing facts, ideas, and details is what makes a listener effective. The way to secure enough details is to ask enough questions to understand the message behind the words. Every person in the school has a unique view of the world. It helps to place yourself in the picture from the patron's view. Remove distractions and focus on the message being conveyed. If a comment is made that the library program is inflexible, probe further to clarify the definition of "inflexible." For example, one staff member might consider the library inflexible in the hours of operation, or the method teachers have to follow to bring entire classes to the library, or when students can come on passes. A multitude of interpretations evolves from just the term "inflexible," so make sure your understanding is correct; otherwise, you will be fixing something that isn't broken. Listening is important, but hearing the message is critical in a needs analysis. *Listening means taking in the words spoken or written by the contributor, while hearing means grasping and understanding the message he or she is conveying.* The contributor's intent is determined by continuing to question and clarify the message. During a face-to-face analysis, stay mentally alert. It is also critical to keep an open mind and listen for new ideas. The responses can be outlined with illustrations so that the problem or need is understood in enough detail to modify the library program. Most important, listen with feeling and intuition, because students and staff need to know that you care.

Sample Needs Analysis

A needs analysis can be performed in a variety of ways. Depending on the time available, collecting data in more than one way or triangulating the data is helpful. Three information collection methods that are cheap, easy, and quick are *focus groups*, *interviews*, and *questionnaires*. Face-to-face needs analysis is often effective with small focus groups or with individuals. Each information collection method has advantages and disadvantages.

The advantage of focus groups and interviews is that they require few people and are good methods to begin collecting information that will be used in a more detailed survey to a larger group of people. In interviews and focus groups, questions can be modified to probe deeper or to explore unexpected issues. A focus group provides an opportunity for the respondents to interact, discuss, and clarify the questions. The disadvantage of interviews and focus groups is that the sampling group is usually small and the results might have to be backed up with observation or data. Another disadvantage is that the interviewee can intentionally or unintentionally bias the answers.

A questionnaire is a paper or computerized document that presents a set of questions to which a person responds. Questionnaires should be sent to a representative sample of people. The advantage of the questionnaire is that respondents remain anonymous if they wish. A survey should be short and limited to no more than 15 minutes' completion time. An example of a questionnaire developed through these means is available in appendix B ("Needs Analysis Survey").

Another option that provides immediate and ongoing information is a *computer survey*. This might be more time consuming and costly to set up, depending on available technology support. There are many application and Web-based software programs available that provide assessment if in-house technology personnel are not available.

A Creative Approach

A different approach to conducting a needs analysis is a workshop where small groups composed of administrators, faculty, and students draw a picture depicting their perception of a successful library program (see the needs analysis workshop in appendix C). In this activity the groups can use only pictures (not words or numbers) to explain their drawing. After completing the pictures, ask each group to present and explain their illustrations to the entire group. From the completed drawings, common learning needs of the library stakeholders emerge. Valuable information will be gained from the pictures, the presentations, and the group discussion. Using a flip chart, track the information as the groups convey what their pictures represent.

One representation of a library program evolved when a group of staff members drew a football field with two teams of players, a goal post, a crowd, and coaches. When they explained the picture, they identified the quarterback as the library media specialist, directing the team or teachers toward the goal line. Furthermore, the library media specialist was defined as accessible to administrators, teachers, students, and parents, assisting them in achieving educational aspirations. The goal line was identified as graduation for every student. The coaches or administrators were on the sidelines providing the basic needs for the team, and the crowd or parents were in the stands cheering the team to cross the goal line. Through this representation the library media specialists clearly understood their role in the education process as viewed by the group.

By using this pictorial needs analysis technique, one school identified the desire for a library program that was accessible, inviting, and relevant. The staff and students wanted library media specialists who were involved in school life and who kept up-to-date on trends and issues in the information field. The pictorial format is effective because it opens discussion in an informal, relaxed, and nonthreatening manner. Through this process, new learning needs are identified, and new goals and objectives can emerge.

Once the library program has been evaluated, the vision and mission have been updated, and a needs assessment is complete, use the rubric in *A Planning Guide for Information Power: Building Partnerships for Learning with School Library Media Program Assessment Rubric for the 21st Century* (AASL 1999) to determine what competencies in learning and teaching, information access and delivery, and program administration are being met and which are not. In the AASL guidebook, each target indicator in the rubric is assessed as basic, proficient, or exemplary. Under each of these assessment divisions, a specific criterion delineates the characteristics of what categorizes the quality level of the library program. The library program goal is to progress from a basic utilitarian program to achieve exemplary performance in all target areas. Step 3 explains how to create a plan to address transforming the program minuses into program pluses. The action plan is based on meshing target indicators from the principles of *Information Power* with the results of the needs analysis. An action plan that focuses on the unique needs of the school makes this customization of the library program possible and ensures its success.

Summary

The NSLMPY award requires that all of the library media program's components of learning and teaching, information access and delivery, and program administration be exemplary. Knowing which elements of the library media program are successful and which elements need improvement provides a starting point for library program improvement. Preliminary information is gathered through self-evaluation by the library staff or the core team. The resulting data are presented to a schoolwide committee that agrees or disagrees with the self-evaluation. Once consensus is reached by the schoolwide team and the core team, a review of the library vision and mission provides direction and focus for the library program. Before creating an action plan, it is important to conduct a successful needs analysis. A needs analysis can be accomplished in a variety of ways, from interviews, to focus group discussions, to questionnaires, to workshop activities. After determining the library users' needs, the final step in the evaluation process is to review and document each target indicator under the principles of *Information Power* according to the rubric in AASL's *A Planning Guide for*

Information Power: Building Partnerships for Learning. Each school and each community is distinctive, so action plans that emerge based on a needs analysis are key to a successful and unique program.

References

American Association of School Librarians (AASL). 1999. *A planning guide for Information Power: Building partnerships for learning with school library media program assessment rubric for the 21st century.* Chicago: American Association of School Librarians/American Library Association.

Senge, Peter. 1992. Building learning organizations. *Journal for Quality and Participation* (March): 30–39.

Step 3 Analyzing the Results

Once a needs analysis has been conducted, information from the results provides powerful direction for the library media program. When the results are analyzed within the context of user needs, the library media program not only meets but exceeds the expectations of the members of the school community. Success is guaranteed because two principles are fulfilled:

1. Users will return for more services and resources when their needs are satisfied.

2. Elements of the library program become integrated with the curriculum area needs.

Translating user needs into practical library initiatives and services results in a school library program that is fully integrated into the school's curriculum and is central to the learning process (AASL 2004). Analyzing data from the needs analysis provides insight into the level of staff and student understanding about information literacy. It also determines how the library instructional program is affecting curriculum and student learning. A needs analysis will

- identify user expectations,

- determine user needs,

- identify top-performing library program elements,

- indicate weaknesses in library service processes,

- assess user technology needs, and

- provide documentation for funding requests.

A library media program based on a school's needs analysis and integrated with AASL's national standards results in an innovative instructional design that is customized to meet the mission and vision of the school. Application for the NSLMPY award is judged on "how well the mission of the library program is integrated into the mission, goals and objectives, and long range plans of the school community in which it is located" (AASL 2004, n.p.). This chapter focuses on assessment strategies that enable the library media specialist to collect, analyze, and report data that will result in a library media program influenced by user needs, with *Information Power* as its backbone.

Synthesizing the Results

Organizing the results from a needs analysis gives meaning to the information received. First and foremost, the data must be compiled and sorted. Tabulating the answers into the categories of learning and teaching, information access and delivery, and program administration is routine work and can be done by an individual or a group. Computer-driven, paper-driven, and workshop-driven needs analysis are addressed below:

- Computer driven—One advantage of a needs analysis performed via a software program is that the sorting of the data is available as part of the software program.

- Paper driven—Collecting and sorting the data from paper questionnaires and surveys is more time consuming. When working with a paper survey, create a tabulation form from a copy of the survey. A sample needs analysis tabulation form (see appendix B) provides a concise summary of the respondents' needs.

- Workshop driven—When performing a needs analysis through a workshop format, the participants tabulate the results during the workshop.

Place additional comments that are made on the surveys on a chart, noting how frequently each idea is expressed. Highlight the results that have a high frequency in the negative side of the survey. These negative answers indicate that a weakness in the library media program exists. For example, if respondents' answers indicate that the library media specialist *does not* collaborate instructionally with teachers, then collaboration is a weakness that must be addressed. Collaboration is one of the key ingredients in *Information Power* and is an essential element to master when applying for the NSLMPY award.

Agreeing on Identified Needs

The stakeholders should then examine the tabulated needs for agreement. An effective method to ensure the school community's input and consensus on the identified needs is to allow the school community team to review the tabulated concerns. The process begins with the library media staff. They review the tabulated list to reach agreement on the needs expressed. They also prioritize the needs from the library media staff's perspective.

The staff

1. create a list of user needs based on the three principles of *Information Power* (see Figure 4.1);

2. review the list of user needs for accuracy;

3. add items to the list of needs that the staff determine are missing;

4. delete irrelevant, duplicate, and overlapping items; and

5. determine the top two priorities under each of the three *Information Power* principles.

User Needs by *Information Power* Categories

Learning and Teaching

1. Student library skills are integrated into class assignments.

2. The librarian collaborates instructionally with teachers.

3. The librarian is involved in curriculum planning.

4. The librarian's teaching methods are varied and effective.

5. Reading for enrichment and pleasure is encouraged.

6. Students' varied learning styles are well supported.

7. Students develop individual search strategies.

8. Student learning is assessed.

Information Access and Delivery

1. The library accommodates multiple classes.

2. Library print and electronic resources meet my needs.

3. The library environment encourages student use.

4. Access to library resources meets my needs.

5. The library resources are well-balanced in all formats.

6. The principles of intellectual freedom are supported.

7. Ethical issues such as copyright and fair use are implemented.

Program Administration

1. The library staffing is sufficient to meet user needs.

2. The library staff communicates with department heads regularly.

3. Useful professional development workshops are provided.

4. Library materials are accessible and easy to find.

Figure 4.1. User needs by *Information Power* categories.

An example of a library staff's prioritized list is shown in Figure 4.2.

Library Teams' Prioritized Needs by *Information Power* Categories

Learning and Teaching

1. Reading for enrichment and pleasure is encouraged.

2. The librarian collaborates instructionally with teachers.

Information Access and Delivery

1. Library print and electronic resources meet my needs.

2. Access to library resources meets my needs.

Program Administration

1. The library staff communicates with department heads regularly.

2. Useful professional development workshops are provided.

Figure 4.2. Library teams' prioritized needs by *Information Power* categories.

Next the school community team reviews the tabulated list to reach agreement on the needs expressed. They also prioritize the needs from their perspective.

The school community team

1. reviews the list of user needs based on the three principles of *Information Power* (see Figure 4.1);

2. adds items to the list of needs that the school community team determines are missing;

3. deletes irrelevant, duplicate, and overlapping items; and

4. determines the top two priorities under each of the three *Information Power* principles.

An example of a school community's prioritized list is shown in Figure 4.3 (p. 44).

School Community Team's Prioritized Needs
by *Information Power* Categories

Learning and Teaching

1.   Reading for enrichment and pleasure is encouraged.

2.   The librarian's teaching methods are varied and effective.

Information Access and Delivery

1.   Access to library resources meets my needs.

2.   The library resources are well-balanced in all formats.

Program Administration

1.   The library staff communicates with department heads regularly.

2.   Useful professional development workshops are provided.

**Figure 4.3. School community team's prioritized needs
by *Information Power* categories.**

The final step is to compare the top two prioritized needs from the library team (see Figure 4.2) with the top two prioritized needs from the school community team (see Figure 4.3) and identify commonalities, note inconsistencies, and choose priorities for the library media program.

Figures 4.2 and 4.3 show the following common elements in the two teams' results. Both teams considered the following important:

- Learning and Teaching—Reading for enrichment and pleasure is encouraged.

- Information Access and Delivery—Both chose access to the library resources as important.

- Program Administration—Both teams chose communication with staff as a top priority, followed by the need for useful staff development as the second priority.

The following inconsistencies in the two teams' results appeared:

- Learning and Teaching—The library staff desired greater collaboration, while the school community was more interested in improving the teaching methods used to deliver instruction.

- Information Access and Delivery—Both chose different needs, but the concerns were similar, indicating that library resources were important to each group.

Next, the teams discuss the results and agree on which needs to focus on improving (priorities):

- Learning and Teaching—Reading for enrichment and pleasure is encouraged.

- Information Access and Delivery—Access to library resources meets student and staff needs.

- Program Administration—The library staff communicate with department heads regularly.

Reviewing the commonalities, noting the inconsistencies, and choosing priorities for the library media program is simplified through this method. It provides a systematic process for synthesizing a large number of identified needs. The condensed needs then can be prioritized into an action plan.

Creating Goals

Once the needs have been prioritized, determine goals and objectives for each identified need. For example, if the school community team and the library team decide that the prioritized need for greater access to materials is the first goal to address, then the teams should begin by asking the question, "What processes or procedures will fulfill this need?" *A process refers to a change in method, while a procedure requires a change to policy.*

The goal to achieve greater student access falls under the principle of Information Access and Delivery in *Information Power*. Target indicator number 3 under information access and delivery in *A Planning Guide for Information Power* is flexible, and equitable access is ensured (AASL 1999). So the goal is that "access to the library media center and its resources is fully flexible and available both during and beyond the school day" (AASL 1999, 38).

The following example explains how an award-winning library creatively addressed the need for greater student access resulting from a student survey. Since achieving more access was a top priority for the students and therefore for the library media program, the library staff and committee came up with three solutions. Each resolution answered the question, "What processes or procedures will fulfill this need?" Note which of the three solutions proposed is a process and which a procedure issue.

- **Process**—Provide a drop box so that materials could be returned faster during the school day and after the library was closed. (This requires a change in the way materials are returned.)

- **Procedure**—Allow students to use the library during lunch without a pass. (This requires a change in policy.)

- **Procedure**—Provide extended hours for student research. (This requires a change in policy.)

The school community team analyzed each idea for practicality and determined that

1. *the drop box* requires money and manpower for installation,

2. *the use of the library during lunch* without passes requires a backup plan in case too many students overload the library, and

3. the *extended hours* require compensation for the library media specialist for working additional hours.

The team investigated the availability and cost of a drop box, created a back-up plan for lunch access, and determined a compensation plan for the extended hours' initiative. Armed with data from parent and student surveys, the access solutions were presented to the principal for approval. The results are summarized below:

1. *Drop Box*—The expense for the drop box was minimal, and the principal approved funds to purchase and install a drop box without hesitation.

2. *Lunch Access*—The library staff decided to allow free and open access to the library during lunch but developed a back-up plan to limit lunch use by issuing passes in the morning to any student if the crowd became too large. (After 10 years, the back-up plan is still unnecessary. Approximately 400 students spend their lunch time in the library as a result of the no-pass option, but the library media specialists find the orderly usage by students makes a pass system unnecessary.)

3. *Extended Hours*—The library media specialists surveyed the students to determine how late to extend the library hours and the most suitable day of the week. The students chose to keep the library open until six o'clock in the evening. The library media specialist devised a rather creative compensation solution. With administrative approval, the library media specialist received compensation time for the three and a half extended hours. The compensation solution allowed the library media specialists to use the built-up leave at times designed to minimize any negative impact on staff and students. For example, the library media specialist often schedules leave during schoolwide testing times and assemblies.

Increased access continues to be a priority for this library. As soon as online database sources evolved, the library media specialist collected data from CD-ROM usage statistics to justify additional funding for purchasing Web-based subscriptions. The staff and students supported the request because everyone benefits from library resources. In addition to home access to Web-based databases and catalog resources, students and staff continue to gain greater access to resources from the library.

AASL defines an exemplary library media program as one in which "access to the library media center and its resources is fully flexible and available both during and beyond the school day" (AASL 1999). These three access solutions raised the library program from proficient to exemplary. Programs that qualify for the National School Library Media Program of the Year Award should be exemplary in all areas.

Creating a Plan

A plan to create positive change must have the buy-in of the various stakeholders. Those affected will support and promote change if they are a part of the planning process. The following is a streamlined process for creating an action plan:

1. State the user need.

2. Show where the need intersects with *Information Power.*

3. Create a goal based on *Information Power.*

4. Brainstorm objectives to solve the need.

5. Create the tools to implement the initiative.

6. Test the tools.

7. Revise the plan.

8. Implement the solution globally.

9. Evaluate the plan after three months.

10. Revise and update as needed.

Following is an example of how this plan of action can work using the team priority under Learning and Teaching to encourage reading for enrichment and pleasure.

State the user need: Reading for enrichment and pleasure is encouraged.

Show where it intersects with *Information Power*: Learning and Teaching principle number 6 (see appendix A), indicator 5.

Create a goal based on *Information Power*: Develop a schoolwide reading program to encouraging reading for enrichment and personal pleasure.

Brainstorm objectives to solve the need:

1. Share a common reading experience.

2. Encourage interdisciplinary connections and curriculum sharing.

3. Experience meaningful learning through reading.

4. Open a dialog among members of the school community.

5. Design activities to support the learning standards.

6. Understand that a work of fiction can be a parable and an opportunity for people to read and discuss deep issues.

Create the tools to implement the initiative:

1. Create a fact sheet with the mission, objectives, and a projected time line.

2. Create a book selection committee to identify a lead book and companion books.

3. Create a tool kit containing discussion questions, curriculum connections, and evaluation tools.

4. Present the goal to the school leadership for approval.

5. Present the project to the entire school for approval.

Test the tools: Begin using each tool with a leadership team and document what works and what does not work with each. Pilot the project with one grade level.

Revise the plan: Use data from the evaluation tools to make changes and revisions.

Implement the solution globally: Implement the project schoolwide.

Evaluate the plan after three months: Using the evaluation tools and input from staff and students, make final recommendations for the next implementation.

Revise and update as needed: Revise the plan, documents, and implementation as needed.

This planning process enables the school community to understand the connections among user need, *Information Power* standards, and program initiatives. Developing an implementation plan provides an opportunity for the school community to take ownership in the new library goals.

When creating an action plan, sometimes the answers will not come as easily as they did in the illustration of the reading initiative or the issue of greater access to the library media center. The next chapter provides insight into and processes to use when resistance to change surfaces.

Summary

When results from a needs analysis are examined within the context of user needs, the library media program can not only meet but exceed the expectation of the members of the school community. A needs analysis will identify user expectations, determine user needs, identify top-performing library program elements, indicate weaknesses in library service processes, assess user technology needs, and provide documentation for funding requests. The data must be compiled and sorted by tabulating the answers into the categories of learning and teaching, information access and delivery, and program administration. The tabulated needs are then examined by the stakeholders for agreement. The library staff and the school community teams review the tabulated list to reach agreement and to prioritize the needs from their unique perspectives. Next the school community team and the library team decide which prioritized need to undertake first, determine solutions to address the need, and begin a corrective plan to address the need. A streamlined process for creating an action plan includes stating the user need, showing where the need intersects with *Information Power,* creating a goal based on *Information Power,* brainstorming objectives to solve the need, creating the tools to implement the initiative, testing the tools, revising the plan, implementing the solution globally, evaluating the plan after three months, and revising and updating the plan as needed.

References

American Association of School Librarians (AASL). 1999. *A planning guide for Information Power: Building partnerships for learning with school library media program assessment rubric for the 21st century.* Chicago: American Association of School Librarians/American Library Association.

————. 2004. *National School Library Program of the Year award application.* Chicago. Available at: http://www.ala.org/ala/aasl/ aaslawards/natlslmprogram/2005nslmpyapp.pdf (accessed July 14, 2004).

Step 4

Identifying and Overcoming Barriers

Aligning a library media program with *Information Power* is imperative to achieving the NSLMPY award. Often this alignment mandates improvements and changes to the program. Barriers, or roadblocks, arise when change interferes with set beliefs. Because most schools are bureaucracies, the school staff are often guided by the belief that changes create a negative realignment of power and a shift of resources from one program to another. Thus, teachers anticipate loss of power, money, and resources when changes to any program are initiated. Resistance from teachers creates barriers that must be addressed proactively.

Negative reactions to library program initiatives are minimized when teachers, administrators, students, and parents join with the library media specialist to evaluate and analyze the library program. The library media specialist helps the school community-represented team visualize the library program of the *Information Power* era. A gentle, systematic urging, framed in the context of providing better services, creates new library awareness for the school library user. The library media specialist who follows the process outlined in this book is leading by being led.

Throughout the library evaluation process, the committee members, acting as spokespersons for segments of the school community, sign off on each change that is consistent with the goals of *Information Power*. During the committee process the library media specialist redirects committee suggestions that are incompatible with the principles of *Information Power* by implying, hinting, or suggesting. This leadership style minimizes the anxiety, sense of loss, and fear surrounding change. It also provides an avenue for an improved library media program that is eligible for the NSLMPY award.

Change Theory

To further understand how and why barriers to change occur, Michael Fullan's educational change theory explains the underlying factors affecting change in schools. Fullan claims that there are no hard-and-fast rules guiding change due to the contingencies surrounding specific local situations. This is attributed to the fact that no two school communities are alike, and multiple variables interact within a community, affecting the initiation of change (Fullan 2001, 49).

Table 5.1 outlines eight possible factors affecting change in education. According to Fullan, these factors can affect the initiation of change independently or in combination with one or more other factors. Change in the library for the purpose of winning the NSLMPY award is more than likely a consequence of factor 7, the need for funding, combined with factor 8, problem solving and bureaucratic orientations. The desire to achieve recognition as the number one school library media center in the country, combined with a monetary award in the thousands of dollars, is an extremely effective initiator of change.

Implementing Change

Michael Fullan notes that once change is initiated, *need, clarity, complexity,* and *quality/practicality* are factors that affect the implementation of change (2001, 72). The school community will respond positively to any change that meets their personal needs and will object strongly to any change that does not. That is why it is important to ensure that through a library committee process, the desires of individuals within the school are openly discussed and examined. Teachers, administrators, and students must be convinced that implementation of changes to the library program will not impede their funding, time, and resource requests.

"*Clarity* (about goals and means) is a perennial problem in the change process" (Fullan 2001, 76). *Clarity* is accomplished though committee communication and staff training. Committee communication is enhanced and expanded through a systematic training plan for all staff. Educating the key players in the best practices of an award-winning library program must occur first. Then, the library media specialist collaborates with these key players to train the entire staff. Continuous training occurs as new staff members and administrators join the school.

Table 5.1. Factors Affecting Initiation (Phase I)
of the Change Process in Education

Factor	Description/Examples
1. Existence and Quality of Innovations	New body of knowledge with regard to best practices in the field of library media. Examples include national standards as published in *Information Power*; instructional models (Big Six, the I-Search Process, or Pathways to Knowledge by Follett); and Web-based databases.
2. Access to Innovation	National and state library professional organizations' conferences and publications, listserv, vendor support, and local partnerships in which information and opportunities for innovations are shared can contribute to initiation.
3. Advocacy from Central and/or School Administration	Interest from state or local level supervisors, district superintendent, or school principal can provide internal authority, support, and access to internal and external resources that can affect initiation.
4. Teacher Advocacy	Successful library use by an individual teacher can stimulate initiation through word of mouth to other teachers. Improved student projects, ease in locating information, and library support for planned lessons all contribute to teacher advocacy.
5. External Change Agents	National and local accrediting agencies and state legislative initiatives generate library program change.
6. Community Pressure/ Support/Apathy	Reaction or lack of reaction from a community can affect library program change. For example, high-stakes testing, workforce changes, and a conservative or liberal community will affect monetary and philosophical decisions.
7. New Policy and/or Funds (Federal, State, Local)	National, state, and local literacy skills standards can create change. Grants and award funding are stimuli for change. Funding examples include AASL's National School Library Media Program of the Year Award (NSLMPY), AASL's Collaborative School Award, and literacy grants.
8. Problem-Solving and Bureaucratic Orientations	Addressing problems or meeting bureaucratic needs can affect initiation. Examples include cost-saving measures, an opportunity for name recognition, and a desire for external funds.

**Factors adapted from *The New Meaning of Educational Change*
(3rd ed.) by M. Fullan (2001, 54).**

Complexity refers to "alterations in beliefs, teaching strategies, and use of materials" (Fullan 2001, 78). The alteration process begins when the library committee forms and continues throughout the duration of the library program revision and afterward through continual evaluation and adaptation. The success of this process is highly dependent on effective communication and training.

The final factor, which Fullan calls *quality and practicality,* refers to showing the practical need and quality results that change produces (2001, 78). Using proven data, the library media specialist verbalizes the quality results from the many studies of school library media programs spanning the past 40 years. "In research done in nine states and over 3300 schools done since 1999, the positive impact of the school library media program is consistent. Strong school library media programs make a difference in academic achievement" (Lance and Loertscher 2002, 3). The results of these studies indicate that test scores are expected to be 10–20 percent higher in schools that fund strong library media programs (Lance and Loertscher 2002, 23). Inquiry-based class projects, higher level research, and curriculum-rich resources convey that the *Information Power* library is practical and quality driven. The library media specialist needs to address as many factors affecting the implementation of change as possible, for as Fullan states, "the more factors supporting the implementation, the more change in practice will be accomplished" (2001, 71).

Identifying Barriers

Knowing what factors affect the initiation and implementation of change allows the library media specialist to anticipate how and why barriers occur. As each fear surfaces, whether in the initiation or the implementation stage, the library media specialist must effectively investigate and overcome each emerging barrier. The following four steps assist in this process:

1. Brainstorm the causes and effects of the barriers affecting implementation of change.

2. Create a fishbone diagram to provide an organized view of the situation.

3. Use key teachers to analyze the resulting barriers, brainstorm key solutions, and assist in implementing program improvements.

4. Create tools to expedite problems and propel the project ahead.

A fishbone or *Ishikawa diagram*, named after Kaoru Ishikawa, is an effective brainstorming method that provides understanding of the underlying reasons preventing change. The Ishikawa diagram is also called a *cause-and-effect diagram*. The diagram looks somewhat like a fishbone, with the problem defined in the center. The bones growing out of the spine list possible causes of the problem (Shashkin and Kiser 1993, 173). Depending on the school and the school system, different causes prevent positive program changes. Analyzing the barriers by means of a fishbone diagram provides an individualized critique for each roadblock.

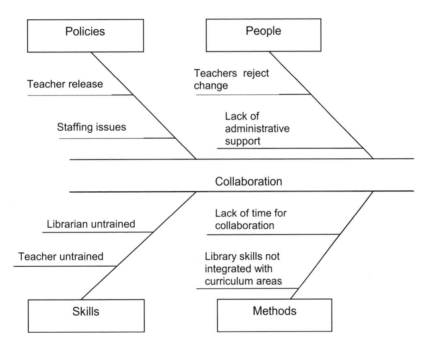

**Figure 5.1. This diagram illustrates probable reasons
why collaboration is not occurring.**

Figure 5.1 is a fishbone diagram that explores the problems an elementary school librarian encountered when trying to implement collaboration. Collaboration is essential to earning the NSLMPY award because it is a requirement for the integrated library media program philosophy promoted by *Information Power*. "As Information Specialist, the library media specialist working collaboratively with teachers, administrators, and parents engages in the developmental process with the planning team, using knowledge of school curriculum and professional resources" (American Library Association 1994). The diagram shows the policies, people, skills, and methods preventing acceptance of collaboration in the elementary school.

The fishbone diagram provides an organized view of why collaboration is being challenged by the teachers in the school. The spine states the problem, which in this case is lack of collaboration. The bones identify four causes: policies, people, skills, and methods that are preventing collaboration from occurring. The smaller bones identify major issues in each causal category. For collaboration to become a reality, each of these issues must be assessed. Although examining each causative issue in a fishbone diagram seems overwhelming, it is easier to create change when the obstacles are defined and thought through carefully.

The example in Figure 5.1 shows that teacher release and staffing policies are hindering the initiation and implementation of collaboration. In addition, people issues such as lack of administrative support and teacher acceptance for change is also negatively affecting collaboration initiatives. Administering collaboration requires specific training for the library media specialist and the teachers. Another roadblock, insufficient time, discourages collaboration, resulting in library skills that are taught in isolation.

Following is a more detailed explanation of each barrier preventing the implementation of collaboration.

Policies

- **Concern: Teacher release.** Teachers use their planning time to plan collaboratively with the library media specialist. It is necessary to address the teachers' need to feel compensated for losing this time.

- **Concern: Staffing issues.** The library media specialist needs staffing assistance to provide time to plan with teachers on various grade levels while continuing to fulfill individualized research, teaching, collection development, technology management, checkout, and clerical responsibilities.

People

- **Concern: Teachers reject change.** The loss of planning time creates anxiety and fear.

- **Concern: Lack of administrative support.** The administration prefers dealing with one unhappy library media specialist rather than 40 upset teachers.

Skills

- **Concern: Librarian untrained.** Since collaboration is not the norm in the district, the library media specialist needs a model to implement collaboration.

- **Concern: Teacher untrained.** Undergraduate and postgraduate education programs do not include training on how to collaborate with the library media specialist to integrate curriculum with library research.

Methods

- **Concern: Lack of time for collaboration.** The teachers' perception is that no time is available to meet with the library media specialist. Teachers fear that collaborative planning is too time consuming.

- **Concern: Library skills not integrated with curriculum areas.** Without collaboration, library skills are taught in isolation because the classroom curriculum connection is unavailable. Research shows that teaching competencies in isolation is not effective for the retention and transfer of skills.

Brainstorming Solutions

After brainstorming the concerns affecting the initiation of collaboration, the library media specialist in this particular elementary school realized that it would be easier to convince two grade levels to begin collaborating rather than to change the entire school all at once. If a few grade levels in the school tried collaborating and succeeded, then the entire school paradigm might change. The library media specialist first talked with the principal and explained that she wished to provide the students with more information literacy lessons integrated into the curriculum standards. More integrated lessons required that planning time between staff and the library media specialist be provided. The principal fully supported the concept and agreed to back the library media specialist; however, the principal refused to meet with the teachers to help initiate the change. In essence, if the library media specialist could convince the teachers to try collaboration, then the principal would also support the change.

The library media specialist then approached one teacher on each of two grade levels, and the teachers together with the library media specialist brainstormed solutions to the barriers preventing the implementation of collaboration. A summary of the solutions for overcoming the existing barriers follows.

Policies

- **Concern: Teacher release.**

  - **Resolution:** With collaboration, the teachers spend their planning time planning integrated library lessons with the library media specialist. To compensate, the library media specialist offers to provides one fixed 15-minute block each week for students to check out books. This provides a break for teachers on days when they have no planning.

- **Concern: Staffing issues.**

  - **Resolution:** The library media specialist schedules unencumbered time to facilitate meeting with teams during the team planning time.

People

- **Concern: Teachers reject change.**

  - **Resolution:** By selling collaboration to one teacher on each grade level, the library media specialist could then use these teachers' acceptance to present the idea to their teams. The teachers asked their teams about additional concerns.

- **Concern: Lack of administrative support.**

  - **Resolution:** It is important to present data on the academic benefits of collaboration. In addition, in her conversation with the principal about the direction of the library media program, the desire for change, and the need for the program to be in compliance with AASL national standards, the library media specialist provided important information in support of collaboration and ended the conversation by mentioning the opportunity to bring funding to the school through AASL-sponsored awards such as the NSLMPY award.

Skills

- **Concern: Librarian untrained.**

  - **Resolution:** The library media specialist reads *Information Power,* attends state professional conferences, contacts the state's school library media professional organization, and requests that AASL provide a list of local members, professional readings, and logistical assistance. Visits to schools that implement collaboration are made, and the library media specialist asks for guidance in scheduling, planning, and teaching collaboratively.

- **Concern: Teacher untrained.**

  - **Resolution:** The library media specialist constructs a calendar and joint planning form to help the teachers visualize collaborative efforts. The calendar provides a representation of library availability and time for team planning. The joint planning form defines the collaborative project, identifies teacher needs, and assesses student needs. The library media specialist uses each grade level meeting as a training opportunity for these tools.

Methods

- **Concern: Lack of time for collaboration.**

  - **Resolution:** The library media specialist agreed to join the grade-level teachers during their team planning. Prior to the team meeting, the library media specialist requests topics and concepts being considered by the team for student study and research. Armed with preresearched material, the library media specialist helps to define a suggested library project.

- **Concern: Library skills not integrated into curriculum areas.**

  - **Resolution:** The library media specialist attends the grade level meeting when the project is discussed, identifies the information literacy skills necessary to complete the project, and then teaches these skills to the students. The skills are introduced on the initial library visit. The information literacy skills are reinforced and new skills stressed on each subsequent visit until the project is completed.

Action Plan

Once the selected teachers and the library media specialist resolve each concern on paper, then the library media specialist is ready to further implement change by meeting with teachers at each of the two grade levels. This meeting is less intimidating because the library media specialist knows what the teachers' needs are after brainstorming using the fishbone diagram. In addition, through problem solving with the selected teachers, the teachers' goals are now clear. It is time to address Fullan's issue of *complexity,* in which alteration of the teachers' beliefs, teaching strategies, and use of the library will begin. Approaching the individual teams with one member of each grade level supporting the change provides confidence and support for the library media specialist.

The library media specialist should begin the meeting by asking the grade level teachers if they would like to improve student comprehension of curriculum standards and improve the quality of their students' research projects and critical thinking skills. Most teachers will welcome the reinforcement of classroom curriculum concepts and skills. Then the library media specialist should illustrate how collaboration improves student learning by comparing student projects collaboratively planned with student projects planned in isolation.

A unit researching the impact of the Olympics on history provides a concrete example of the problems surrounding research without collaboration. The first major hindrance to completing any project without collaboration is that the students' focus is blurred without clear expectations from the teacher. In addition, the projects are based on research purposes rather than curriculum standards. For example, without collaboration, the teacher introduces the unit in the classroom, but the library media specialist is unaware what concepts the students in the class are required to research. Since library time is preplanned by the library media specialist, information literacy skills are introduced without the benefit of incorporating them into an authentic learning situation for the students. In the case of the Olympics project, the library media specialist might use the ancient games as the focus for student learning while the teacher is emphasizing the impact of science on Olympic sports. With collaboration the focus is clear, and the students' learning is an active information skills experience that reinforces concepts assessed in the classroom.

The team meeting should end with the library media specialist addressing each teacher's concern effectively as a result of brainstorming with key players affected by the change. The teams should agree to try collaboration based on a well-constructed plan that creates positive support for the initiation factors *need, clarity, and complexity.* By using the fishbone diagram to identify and brainstorm solutions, the elementary library media specialist discussed above successfully implemented collaboration. Any library media specialist can replicate this process to overcome barriers and create positive program change. Each situation will have somewhat different barriers and solutions to the problem of implementing collaboration.

Creating Tools

When implementing collaboration, the joint planning form, library calendar, lesson plan, and evaluation process are basic tools that will assist any library media specialist in addressing concerns about time as well as clarifying issues regarding instructional roles. In addition, these tools provide positive public relations and excellent documentation of collaboration. These tools are evidence that the library media program is in compliance with the principles of *Information Power* and lend credibility to the library program when applying for the NSLMPY award.

The joint planning form (see appendix B) is a one-page sheet on which the librarian and teacher fill in basic information about (a) what the purpose of the library visit is, (b) when the class will be coming to the library, (c) where the project connects with the library and the curriculum area, and (d) how long students will need to accomplish successful research. This planning form is a tremendous time saver and facilitates linkage between classroom curriculum and library skills. Faculty can fill out this form at a time that is convenient to them. The library media specialist can look over the form, reflect on the needs of the teacher and students to complete the project, and respond to the teacher. Two joint planning forms are available in appendix B.

A library calendar serves as an organizational tool (see appendix B). It depicts the library schedule visually and helps with management of space, time, and information resources. The calendar should show the day clearly and address the coordination of specific jobs related to teaching and learning, information access and delivery, and program administration. For example, the library media specialist indicates on the calendar when processing, acquisitions, instruction, collaboration, and assessments are planned.

Creating an individual lesson plan for each class that visits the library is critical evidence that the library media specialist is a teacher (see appendix B). Each lesson plan clarifies the role of the library media specialist and the role of the teacher. The lesson plan identifies the instructional standards to be taught and focuses on student information literacy skills necessary to accomplish the teacher-generated assignment. This serves as a teaching guide for the library media specialist. The library media specialist then attaches the library plan to the joint planning form and the teacher project sheet. Copies are made for the teacher, administrators, and library media specialist.

It is important to have a tool that evaluates the completed lesson. One of the simplest evaluations is to ask the teacher and selected students what went well and what needed improvement with the lesson and library time. A more elaborate form or rubric can be used as the faculty become more comfortable with the collaboration process. See appendix B for a collaborative teaching evaluation form.

A school that is a viable candidate for the NSLMPY award supports that claim with documentation and statistics that the library program is fully integrated into the curriculum. This means that there is factual, statistic-driven evidence that information literacy standards are integral to the curriculum, and that collaborative planning, curriculum development, and collaborative teaching are routine *and* essential to the daily operation of the library media program. The joint planning form, library calendar, lesson plan, and evaluation documentation prove that *Information Power's* principles of teaching and learning are implemented.

Summary

Aligning a library media program with *Information Power* is imperative to achieving the NSLMPY award. Often this alignment mandates improvements and changes to the program. Preparation for change requires an understanding of change theory as well as an understanding of the factors affecting the initiation and implementation of change. Underlying fears and anxiety create barriers. These barriers, or roadblocks, are surmountable if explored for cause and effect.

- Brainstorm the causes and effects of the barriers to implementation of change.

- Create a fishbone diagram to provide an organized view of the situation.

- Use key teachers to analyze the resulting barriers, brainstorm key solutions, and assist in implementing program improvements.

- Create tools to expedite problems and propel the project forward.

Collaboration is encouraged when tools make it easier and convenient for the faculty to work with the library media specialist. Effective tools that address time and communications issues are a joint planning form, a library calendar, a sample library literacy lesson plan, an evaluation plan, and a training plan. These tools are time savers that assist in identifying instructional roles as well as instructional needs.

References

American Library Association. 1994. *Position statement on the role of the library media specialist in outcomes-based education.* Chicago. Available at: http://www.ala.org/ala/aasl/aaslproftools/positionstatements/aaslpositionstatementrolelibrary.htm (accessed September 20, 2004).

Fullan, Michael. 2001. *The new meaning of educational change.* 3rd ed. New York: Teachers College Press.

Lance, Keith Curry, and David V. Loertscher. 2002. *Powering achievement: School library media programs make a difference: the evidence mounts.* 2nd ed. San Jose, CA: Hi Willow Research & Publishing.

Shashkin, Marshall, and Kenneth J. Kiser. 1993. *Putting total quality management to work: What TQM means, how to use it and how to sustain it over the long run.* San Francisco: Berrett-Koehler Publishers.

Step 5 Developing Training Modules

New policies and procedures, initiated with proper training, ensure successful implementation of library program initiatives. Training makes certain that everyone in an organization has a common understanding about a new policy, process, or program. It is an opportunity for key people to hear the same information at one time. When introducing initiatives, the library media specialist will benefit from communicating important guidelines via staff development because it saves time, ensures quality, and provides consistency.

Teachers and administrators do not typically learn about library best practices in higher education courses. Collaborating with the library media specialist is not usually a part of teacher or administration certification coursework. Working with a library media specialist is most often the result of on-the-job training. When the library media specialist makes professional development a keystone of the library media program, then the staff will draw from new information rather than previous experiences. Without training, the teaching and administrative staff's library experiences, which include both disturbing as well as cherished library encounters, will dictate library use.

Communicating *Information Power* to the staff is hampered by many factors, as evidenced by a study of the Chicago public schools. The observations concluded that:

> Only about one-third of the teachers in the system engage in regular dialogue about instruction. One-quarter, work in schools where teachers and administrators disagree about school goals and norms of practice. Half fail to see any real coherence and continuity across programs in their schools. Most believe that their schools have so many programs coming and going that they cannot keep track of them all. (Fullan 2001, 253)

Without instructional dialogue to clarify the library media program goals, staff will maintain the status quo rather than attempt to incorporate new ideas and methods into their already full agenda. Professional development opportunities open dialogue and convey library media program goals through face-to-face opportunities. This develops a relationship between the staff and the library media specialist.

Providing training increases acceptance of the library program. Training is essential when applying for the NSLMPY award. Principle 8 under program administration in *Information Power* states that, "ongoing staff development—both to maintain professional knowledge and skills and to provide instruction in information literacy for teachers, administrators, and other members of the learning community—is an essential component of the library media program" (ALA and AECT 1998, 110). This chapter explains how to design and deliver effective training in the school setting.

Designing Training

Teachers, like students, need just-in-time training that provides clarity, synthesis, practice, collaboration, and evaluation. The objectives for the training bring clarity by conveying the purpose for the session. In turn, the participants must be able to relate the information from the session to their particular needs. They also need opportunity to practice the new skill. Using group work as part of the training opportunity emphasizes collaboration and provides additional practice. All training sessions should permit the participants to provide evaluation and feedback about the presentation and the usefulness of the session.

When designing professional development sessions for the staff, it is important to remember that effective training involves the elements of *time, audience, creativity*, and *style*. In the school setting, time is limited and the audience is composed of teachers who are trainers themselves. Using creativity when designing training encourages retention, and an appropriate delivery style provides structure. Understanding the importance of each element increases the opportunity for a successful in-service.

Time is a scarce commodity for teachers and administrators. Structuring training within the school day is preferable. Blocks of time for teacher training are identified by examining the school schedule. Usually training time is available before school, after school, during planning blocks, or during team meetings. The library media specialist who creates a series of short training sessions that focus on developing one aspect of the library program validates the staff's time concerns. By repeating short 20- to 30-minute training sessions during the day, teachers are provided with multiple opportunities to be a part of the information-sharing session. Access to training that is flexible and varied respects teachers' time constraints.

Knowing your *audience* considers the participants' learning needs. When creating a professional development plan, understand that

- teachers are adult learners,

- individual teacher needs must be balanced with the needs of the library program,

- program components that are practical and utilitarian will be accepted faster,

- teachers need ongoing support during and after the professional development, and

- activities should provide opportunity for experimentation and reflection.

When developing training sessions, refer to these points and check each item to ensure that teachers' learning needs are validated.

Creativity sparks curiosity, motivation, and new ways of thinking. Effective training includes appropriate, well-thought-out, and intellectually challenging materials that are presented creatively. Activities that stimulate the senses of sight, sound, smell, taste, and touch appeal to the creative side of participants' brains. Presenting new policies and procedures by using varied activities prevents boredom and ensures greater attention to the information.

An active learning *style* increases retention of information during training. When using participatory activities, the attendees take more responsibility for their learning. Active learning affords practice in the skills needed for a specific task or outcome. When developing activities, first identify the purpose for the assignment and then evaluate whether the activity will enhance the understanding of the topic. For example, a session conveying the importance of collaboration is an opportunity to present the participants with a task in which teamwork is important to the outcome. The following activity illustrates how a team activity typifies collaboration. The "destination activity" is a puzzle; participants are given a starting point with five simple but mixed-up street directions and asked to determine the destination. This activity is almost impossible to solve. Yet if the participants are provided with the opportunity to work in groups, often the puzzle is solved quickly because the directions become clear through teamwork. This activity illustrates that collaboration on a project between the library media specialist and the classroom teacher results in meaningful research. See appendix C for instructions for this activity.

Effective staff development not only considers the elements of time, audience, creativity, and style but also accomplishes set goals and objectives based on needs. For example, if the need is to provide participants with an effective communication tool to encourage collaboration, then create a training session that is short, practical, creative, and activity driven. The joint planning forms found in appendix B are examples of a communication tool that promotes collaboration. In addition, the forms identify where the library skills are integrated into the curriculum. A joint planning form explains available resources and clarifies the learning objectives for curriculum projects. Students' learning needs are also identified using such a form. Explaining the information documented on the joint planning form to staff members shows the practical and utilitarian nature of the tool. As teachers become familiar with the form, they will understand that the students' learning needs are expedited because the time spent on projects is streamlined and focused. Instruction on how to use the joint planning form can be enhanced by activities such as conducting a mock interview between the library media specialist and a teacher. This interview should be followed by having participants practice using the tool with each other. This practice during training shows how easy the tool is to use. Teachers who are comfortable with the tool will incorporate the form into their day-to-day plans.

Delivering Training

Once a professional development session has been created, the library media specialist should consider the best way to deliver the training. Although it is often necessary to train an entire staff, the library media specialist isn't obligated to train large numbers at one time. There are different options available to incorporate training into the school setting. Effective formats for delivering training include *collaborative, top-down*, and *document* delivery. Whether providing the training in a large group or smaller concurrent sessions, these models work well for library program training because they utilize the basic principles for an exemplary library program.

Collaborative delivery uses principle 3 under "Learning and Teaching" in *Information Power,* which states that "the library media program models and promotes collaborative planning and curriculum development. (ALA and AECT 1998, 58). The teachers will experience collaboration through meeting with the library media specialist to plan the learning strategies and activities to implement a staff development session. One method of collaborative delivery begins by training the department heads or team leaders on a specific information resource or information literacy concept. The department chairs then suggest curriculum topics to use in the training session. Then the library media specialist suggests which information resources and information literacy skills will best complete the curriculum activity. Working collaboratively, the department chairs and the library media specialist design a session that is targeted to the curriculum teachers' needs. Together the teacher and library media specialist provide the ensuing staff development.

Top-down training is when the leaders of the school are trained first, followed by staff, students, and parents. The purpose of top-down training is to provide the decision makers in the building with valuable resource information that will ultimately assist in planning, developing, and writing curriculum (AASL 1999, 35). When the administrators know how the library staff, resources, and programs promote academic achievement, they will encourage and promote learning that incorporates these resources into the daily life of the school community. Top-down training effectively utilizes administrative leverage and support to promote library initiatives.

Documents transform theory into concrete tools. Theory becomes real when participants are provided with a *handout*, a *software presentation*, a *lesson plan*, or an *experience* that can be referred to for reinforcement. A handout summarizes a concept, method, or key points. Handouts are management tools that monitor and reinforce learning. When providing training about the validity of information on the Internet, a handout with checkpoints that review factors to consider when using Web sites provides guidelines, reinforcement, and practice in using the information from the in-service. Software presentations electronically reproduced provide the training attendees with the opportunity to review the key points of the information given during a training session. A lesson plan developed during an in-service and based on information from the training session allows participants to immediately return to their classes and begin using the new skill with students. Active learning provides the participants with experiences that internalize theory from the in-service. Internalizing information allows attendees to understand the concepts on a deeper, more personal level.

Delivery of training includes validation for the participants. The National Board of Professional Teacher Standards lists five areas that should be validated when delivering training to teachers. Creating professional development opportunities that utilize collaboration, top-down, and document delivery support these five major areas (Fullan 2001, 255–57):

- Teachers are committed to students and their learning.

- Teachers know the subjects they teach and how to teach those subjects to students.

- Teachers are responsible for managing and monitoring students' learning.

- Teachers think systematically about their practice and learn from experience.

- Teachers are members of learning communities.

A school that applies for the NSLMPY award believes that providing training is an effective method of communicating library goals to the school community. *Information Power* maintains that "offering and promoting an ongoing staff development program for the full school community, particularly in the integration of information technology and the use of the information literacy standard for student learning" should be a goal for the school library media specialist" (ALA and AECT 1998, 112). Training is the link between high standards and implementation. A well-trained teaching and administrative staff will assist the library media specialist by passing on new learning skills to students through library use. The library media specialist who takes a leadership role in training the staff is a key agent in enabling teachers and administrators to promote academic success.

Offering training to parents after school and on PTA nights benefits the students and the library program. Extending training to parents creates a greater awareness of library initiatives and educates them about library program needs. The same guidelines for structuring training for staff apply to parent training sessions.

Summary

New policies and procedures, initiated with proper training, ensure successful implementation of library program initiatives. Without training, the teaching and administrative staff's library experiences, which include both disturbing as well as cherished library encounters, will dictate library use. Providing training increases acceptance of the library program, and it is essential when applying for the NSLMPY award. Principle 8 under "Program Administration" in *Information Power* states that "ongoing staff development—both to maintain professional knowledge and skills and to provide instruction in information literacy for teachers, administrators, and other members of the learning community—is an essential component of the library media program" (ALA and AECT 1998, 110). When designing professional development sessions for the staff, it is important to remember that effective training considers the elements of time, audience, creativity, and style. Once a professional development session is created, the library media specialist should consider the best way to deliver the training session. Whether providing the training in a large group or in smaller concurrent sessions, collaborative, top-down, and document delivery all work well for library program training because these methods model the principles for an exemplary program.

References

American Association of School Librarians (AASL). 1999. *A planning guide for Information Power: Building partnerships for learning with school library media program assessment rubric for the 21st century.* Chicago: American Association of School Librarians/American Library Association.

American Library Association (ALA) and the Association for Educational Communications and Technology (AECT). 1998. *Information power: Building partnerships for learning.* Chicago: American Library Association and the Association for Educational Communications.

Fullan, Michael. 2001. *The new meaning of educational change.* 3rd ed. New York: Teachers College Press.

Step 6 Novel Connections

A well-thought-out public relations plan conveys positive information about the library to the school community and the public. Each day the library media center is busy with activities that meet the needs of its users. Often new ideas or novel connections surface for the library media specialist to develop into instructional and advocacy initiatives. Just as routine library media program activities bring substance and credibility to the library, novel connections stimulate usage in a different context. Innovative ideas are excellent opportunities for advocacy. This chapter discusses how to develop a public relations plan based on novel connections.

Efforts to inform all segments of the community about the school library media program are time well spent. A communication plan that explains how the library media program contributes to community goals and objectives results in positive library advocacy. *The library media specialist who correlates every idea, policy, procedure, and program taking place in the library to constituents in the community emphasizes inclusion, proving that the library is for everyone.* This outreach is public relations at its best because the community members become advocates through participation in and awareness of the library media program's initiatives.

When creating a public relations strategy, begin by identifying the key library constituents. Key players in a public relations plan fall into waves of use and influence. The concentric circles in Figure 7.1 place the heaviest users in the core of the circle. As the circles become larger and farther from the center, the direct use is lower, but the sphere of influence is broader.

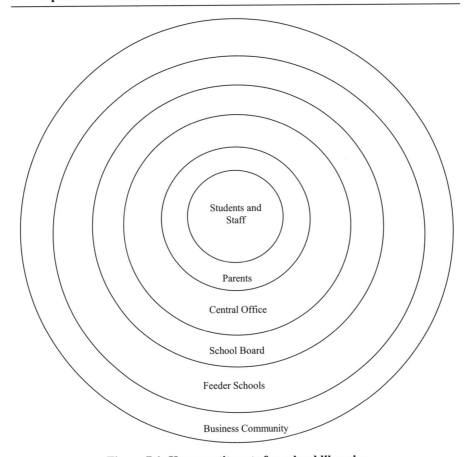

Figure 7.1. Key constituents for school libraries.

An advocacy plan's impact is widened every time each constituent in the diagram is touched by the library program. Successful public relations efforts use a variety of methods to convey information about the library program to as many key players as possible, as often as possible. Public relations is more than press coverage; it is inviting the community to participate in events. This includes inviting constituents to observe, participate in, or contribute to an event. It means making telephone calls, writing thank you notes, and tabulating reports that communicate the library program's contribution to academic achievement.

An effective public relations plan starts with the center core constituents (Figure 7.1) and moves outward toward the business community. Each group of constituents must eventually understand how the library program positively contributes to the learning environment. Advocacy results when the library media program provides a personal connection to the library for each user. From the first day until the last day of the school year, the library media specialist who promotes and documents the program's effectiveness and value for the school community is following principle 9 under "Program Administration" in *Information Power,* which states that, "clear communication of the mission, goals, functions and impact of the library media program is necessary to the effectiveness of the program" (ALA and AECT 1998, 112).

When starting a public relations effort, proactive public relations strategies lie in the hands of the library media specialist. The library media specialist is in the forefront, promoting the library in a positive context. Later teachers, administrators, students, and parents assume an advocacy role.

Key Constituents

Figure 7.1 shows the wide range of people who are reached through an effective public relations plan. Knowing who these people are and how they positively affect a library media program provides motivation to include as many of these constituents as possible in as many activities as possible. The potential connections are endless once the library media specialist recognizes who the key constituents are and how they contribute to the effectiveness of the library program.

The center *core* (or the building level staff and students) are the heaviest users and have the most immediate need for library services. When the library media specialist satisfies their needs, endless public relations opportunities are created. Teachers and students appreciate recognition. Understanding the core constituents' needs for information and validation results in a library media specialist who is welcoming, understanding, and patient. This understanding means that the library media specialist provides the core users with daily doses of practical but essential library services. Opening the library to student displays, student talent, teacher talent, and club events extends the library into the personal lives of individuals.

Communications to *parents* also begin with the first day of each school year and continue throughout the summer months. Use handouts, e-mails, the school Web site, the school newsletter, award presentations, student displays, and other opportunities to disseminate information to parents about how the library is essential to their child's success. Being visible at parent teacher association meetings, sporting events, theater presentations, and band and choral concerts conveys to parents that the library media specialist is interested in their student. Besides being visible, attending these events provides a connection to the students and allows the library media specialist to view students in a different light. In turn, the parents and students view the library program and the library media specialist in a different light.

Central office personnel, including the superintendent, the assistant superintendents, and the educational specialists, should be included when sending invitations to events, copies of memos, and reports about library initiatives. These communications provide a personal connection with each constituent and ensure more intimate understanding of the library media program's needs. The central office personnel are decision makers, and the library media specialist reaps the benefits of keeping them informed when policies are created and funds are distributed.

School board members are child centered. They enjoy involvement in school programs, especially when students are the beneficiaries. Like the central office staff, the school board members base decisions on personal experiences; they visit schools to personalize written policies and see how their decisions affect the students. Every school board member who knows how his or her school libraries contribute to student success will automatically consider the library media specialist's view when voting on issues.

The immediate community comprises *feeder schools.* Including feeder schools in as many initiatives as possible extends the library program's influence because staff and students across grade levels gain a greater understanding of and appreciation for each other. When an elementary library seeks and receives assistance from the middle school and high school in the feeder pattern, the resulting interaction extends deep into the community. As feeder schools work together, they validate each other's programs and advocate for each other.

The *business community* supports school programs with advertising and promotional giveaways. Building library events to spotlight the business community members' unique skills validates their commitment to the school. The library media specialist who invites the business community into the library offers business leaders the opportunity to witness students and staff in the school setting. When identifying business community members, note whether any hold elected positions, because a personal connection with elected officials expands school library awareness at the state and national level. Each person positively affected by the library extends the impact of immediate and future library initiatives.

Media Coverage Tips

When creating a public relations plan, take the time to know your district public relations director. If the district does not have a public relations director, then target all efforts mentioned in this chapter to the local newspaper editor and television station manager. The amount of publicity the library program receives will vary depending on the size of the district and the locality. A good rule of thumb is that for every 30 stories the library sends out, one might be spotlighted in the news. Stories that are newsworthy and attractive to multiple media providers have a better chance for coverage. Some stories are best promoted by a particular medium. For example, an activity that is best described through video is sent to television, whereas a still photo is best promoted to the newspaper. Also, realize that no matter how perfectly timed the story or promotion for the library might be for the community, a major unexpected news event will preempt a school story. If this happens, turn the library event into a feature story that gains interest even when reported after the event takes place.

When pitching a library event, keep the verbiage succinct and focused. Think of your message in terms of a commercial. Then write a news release. Script out ahead of time the answers to who, what, when, where, why, and how. **Who** is doing it? **What** are they doing? **When** are they doing it? **Where** are they doing it? **Why** are they doing it? **How** are they doing it?

A news release is a prepared news story that is written and sent to the public relations director. Designing the news release so that the story is compelling and easily read increases the possibility for coverage. Sending a digital picture taken at the event maximizes the opportunity for news coverage of the library. If the story contains the type of useful information an editor needs, the chance of publication is greater. Be aware that an editor may reprint all or a section of the release as an article. Sometimes editors may use the story as background information for an article already in the works. And if the library is lucky, a journalist may be sent out on assignment for a comprehensive article about the event.

The lead sentence of the news release must contain a *hook* to grab the editor's attention. It should tell what impact the story will have on the community and why the story is newsworthy to the community's target audience. A story that focuses on students, student achievement, or district goals and objectives has a better opportunity for coverage. Always include a contact name and phone number at the bottom of the release so the public relations director can contact someone with information about the event. Follow up by calling the public relations director to ask if the news release was received or if more information is needed. Calling only once keeps from antagonizing the public relations office. It may take several attempts to get coverage, so don't despair if the public relations director can't use every story. Persistence in sending stories out pays off because ultimately the library program receives the exposure it deserves.

Instructional Activities

The most natural public relations opportunities are those with instructional connections that reinforce school and district goals. When promoting the library media program, frame public relations initiatives in light of these goals.

Sometimes routine activities provide the best advocacy. At the beginning of each school year, meet with all teachers and update them on new print and technology resources. Briefing new teachers on the many different resources available to help them with their class plans promotes the library media program for everyday use. Using department chairs, teacher mentors, and other staff to assist with new teacher orientation and with dissemination of information widens the impact of instructional public relations efforts. Serving on curriculum committees and attending departmental meetings, special interest committees, and clubs encourages staff and students to consider the library media program for daily needs. Creating informal programs in which students are attracted to quality reading materials supports school reading initiatives. Throughout the year offering students with opportunities to participate in seasonal promotions that are both literary and research based encourages students to develop information literacy skills.

Following are examples of novel instructional connections that promote the library media program:

- **Schoolwide reading programs**—These reading programs revolve around themes or specific book titles or authors. Media opportunities such as book chats, open forums, and guest speakers should be included when planning the project.

- **Events highlighting student talent**—All curriculum areas of the school are drawn into events when student talent and skills are featured. The student event may be short, informal programs or longer, formal assemblies. Using the Fine Arts Department highlights the chorus, band, art, and photography talents of students. The Science Department can present science experiments that wow students. The Math Department can bring in students from a sports team to explain how geometry is important to success in a sport like tennis, football or basketball.

- **Literary circles**—After choosing a book title for a group to read, bring the students and teachers together in a circle to discuss the book. This is a more formal type of book chat in which teachers in different curriculum areas begin the chat with a lecture on the setting of the book, the historical perspective, the impact of science on the story, or some related topic that adds dimension to the book.

- **Reading poster promotion**—One way to promote reading and encourage teachers and students to share their favorite books and authors is to sponsor an event at which students and teachers are pictured with their favorite books. The pictures are modeled on ALA's read posters and can be printed out in the library and throughout the school. The pictures can also be displayed in kiosk fashion via television or computer.

- **Social events**—Holiday social events sponsored by the library media specialist are promotional opportunities in a relaxed setting where students and faculty discuss issues informally. Coffee and cookies discussions, or festive holiday parties that make use of the school catering department for refreshments, the band for background music, or the chorus for entertainment, emphasize a welcoming, open atmosphere.

- **Instructional promotions**—Scavenger hunts, SAT word-of-the-day challenges, and brainteaser questions often use information literacy skills while reinforcing classroom content. Continue these activities throughout the year by using monthly themes. For example, September can highlight hurricane season; October, the Supreme Court; December, philanthropy; February, heart issues; and March, college basketball.

- **Special collections**—Creating special collections that focus on specific school remembrances adds to the library's collection. A memorial book collection to commemorate the life of a staff member's family, a legacy book collection to focus on student graduates, and a birthday collection to celebrate student and staff birthdays reach out to staff and students by acknowledging memorable events in their lives.

Connecting library activities to a standard, a curriculum area, and a district goal is *always* effective. For example, a novel connection entitled *reading promotion pictures* is a wonderful public relations opportunity because it may include key constituents. In addition, it fulfills principle 6 in *Information Power's* learning and teaching category because it encourages reading and provides open discussion about books and authors. Principle 6 states that, "the library media program encourages and engages students in reading, viewing, and listening for understanding and enjoyment" (ALA and AECT 1998, 66). The reading promotion picture event assists in collection development, which fulfills principle 5 in information access and delivery: "the collections of the library media program are developed and evaluated collaboratively to support the school's curriculum and to meet the diverse learning needs of students" (ALA and AECT 1998, 90). This reading promotion relates to all curriculum areas because students and faculty identify their favorite books based on their interests. Most district goals focus on values such as respect, responsibility, honesty, and accountability, and good literature espouses these values. Therefore, a reading promotion project often supports district goals.

Extending the opportunity for key constituents to participate in the reading poster promotion extends the public relations efforts to wider spheres of community influence (Figure 7.1). The picture poster activity is fun and unites the school through open discussion about books and authors. Inviting central office personnel, school board members, parents, feeder school personnel, and business leaders to participate involves the community in the project. This activity creates an awareness of the importance of books to fulfill lifelong user needs and provides individual recognition for the participants.

Promotional Tips

Getting publicity for an event results from planning. The library's opportunity for coverage may be enhanced by using the following tips. These guidelines make it easier for a media organization to cover library programs.

- Create a press release summarizing the activity and send it to the school system's public relations director well in advance before the program takes place.

- Explore ways to connect the event to local and world events.

- Invite key constituents to participate as soon as the event date is set.

- Involve as many curriculum departments in the event as possible.

- Identify students to assist in planning the project.

- Follow up every activity with thank you notes to key participants.

- Prepare a summary report with pictures of the event and send it to the school administration, central office personnel, school board members, and business leaders.

- Send a follow-up press release explaining the outcomes of the event.

- Send a press release to the student newspaper editor, yearbook editor, school newsletter editor, and school Web master.

Publicity preparation takes place before, during, and after the event. An effective public relations program validates the library media specialist and the library program's contribution to student achievement. It educates all segments of the community about the library media program and satisfies *Information Power*'s mandate to communicate the impact of the library on the school community.

Summary

A well-thought-out public relations plan connects members of the community with the library media program. Advocacy conveys positive information about the library to the school community and the public. When creating a public relations strategy, identify key constituents and then appeal to their needs. The center core or the building level staff and the students are the heaviest users and the constituents with the most immediate need for library services. Parents, central office personnel (including the superintendent, the assistant superintendents, and the educational specialists), school board members, feeder school personnel, and business leaders should be included when sending invitations to events and when sending copies of memos and reports about library initiatives. Meeting with your district public relations director enhances opportunities for promoting the library. If the district does not have a public relations director, then send the information to the newspaper editor or television station manager. When pitching a library event, keep the verbiage succinct and focused by thinking of your message in terms of a commercial. A news release that provides the answers to who, what, where, when, why, and how is effective. When promoting the library media program, frame public relations initiatives in light of school and district goals. An effective public relations program validates the library media specialist and the library program's contribution to student achievement.

References

American Library Association (ALA) and the Association for Educational Communications and Technology (AECT). 1998. *Information power: Building partnerships for learning.* Chicago: American Library Association and the Association for Educational Communications.

Step 7

Applying for the NSLMPY Award

In this day of high-stakes testing, the assessment of the library media program validates the library–classroom connection. When a library media specialist is planning to apply for the NSLMPY award, the chapters of this book will help in building a school library media program that meets the exemplary criteria needed to achieve this award. The library media specialist who completes the steps in this book will create a strategic plan that will result in an improved library media program.

During the strategic planning process, the library media program is evaluated and assessment information is compiled. Although the evaluation of the library media program using AASL's rubric is ongoing, a thorough assessment is now complete. Documentation data for each goal and objective are available and accessible for review. The library media specialist and the school–community committee have identified areas for growth, brainstormed new ideas, and initiated changes based on the school mission. Now the library media specialist, the library staff, and the school–community committee are in an excellent position to apply for the NSLMPY award. This final chapter provides guidance on the application process.

Action Plan

It is imperative to be organized when applying for the NSLMPY award. Developing a time line that targets completion dates for each component of the NSLMPY award application makes the submission process less overwhelming. The following steps sequence the application process:

1. Obtain an application form.

2. Review and clarify the award criteria and rules.

3.   Create a time line.

4.   Collect data.

5.   Elicit staff, student, and community input.

6.   Organize the documentation.

7.   Write a draft description of the program.

8.   Revise and finalize the description of the program.

9.   Fill out the AASL application form.

10.   Mail the application packet before the deadline.

Obtain an award application form to begin the process. There are several methods for acquiring the official application. The library media specialist can request one by writing to AASL or calling the AASL office. The most time-efficient method for securing an application is to access the AASL Web site. Figure 8.1 is a summary of the AASL contact information options.

AASL Contact Information

Mail:
American Association of School Librarians
50 East Huron Street
Chicago, IL 60611-2795

Telephone: 312-280-4382
Toll-free: 1-800-545-2433 ext. 4382
Fax: 312-664-7459

E-mail: aasl@ala.org

Web site: http://www.ala.org/ala/aasl/aaslawards/natlslmprogram/aaslnational.htm

Or: http://www.ala.org and perform a search for:

National School Library Media Program of the Year Award Application

---

Figure 8.1. American Association of School Librarians contact information.

Review and clarify the award criteria and rules to determine whether the library program is qualified to proceed with the application process. The criteria are guidelines that measure the library program and provide insight into how the application is judged. The application material states that there are three criteria for judging the AASL application, which determine

1. "how well the library media program is integrated into the mission, goals and objectives, and long range plans of the school and community in which it is located" (AASL 2004);

2. "how well the library media program carries out its stated mission" (AASL 2004); and

3. the degree to which the program implements the concepts of planning and partnership as described in INFORMATION POWER: *Building Partnerships for Learning*" (AASL 2004).

If the school library program meets the AASL stated criteria, review the application rules. The rules provide explicit definitions, judging guidelines, application requirements, format mandates, mailing suggestions, and required qualifications for the applicants. The rules clarify the category options for a single school, small school district, and large school district. In addition, the rules explain that all applications must be on official forms provided by AASL and must be signed by the superintendent of the school district or division. The size of the paper, print size, spacing, and attachments permitted with the documents are explained in the rules. The application deadline is provided. An important guideline is that "all applicants [sic] must be a current personal member of AASL" (AASL 2004).

Create a time line to ensure that the application is completed on time. The award requires a detailed description of the library media program, signatures of key school personnel, student enrollment data, funding data, library staffing data, and recommendation letters. When creating a time line, start with the end date and work backwards. The process can be completed in three months or less depending on the library media specialist's professional and personal commitments and the school calendar. The time line should include the dates when the data documentation, support letters, program description draft, and final program description are due. For the time line to be effective, time spans should allow time for the material to reach AASL during late December, which is a busy time for the postal service and delivery companies. Figure 8.2 (p. 86) is a sample time line for applying for the NSLMPY award.

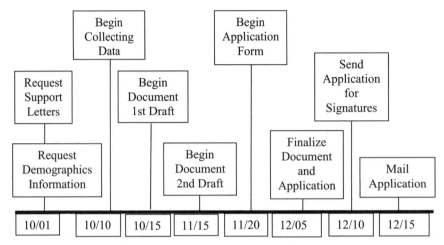

Figure 8.2. Sample time line for applying for the NSLMPY Award.

Collect data before, during, and after writing the program description. The school library media specialist who prepares for the NSLMPY award by using and performing or implementing the suggestions in this book has already collected significant program data. Obtaining additional data pertaining to student enrollment, funding, and library staffing may require district level assistance. Many states and districts provide the school demographics on a school report card. This report card contains information useful for the NSLMPY award application form.

Elicit staff, student, and community input to validate and provide depth to the program description and the application process. Letters of support from teachers, students, and community members establish support for the library while creating an understanding of the importance of the award process. If the time line is tight, ask several different supporters to write letters. Then, if a letter is late, there are still multiple recommendation letters available to submit. Later, when an evaluation committee is sent to the school, these supporters from the school community may assist with the on-site visit.

Organize the documentation for the writing process. When an evaluation committee visits the school, documentation that is collected in a file, crate, box, or cabinet is evidence that support statements in the program description. Electronic files are also useful; however, many documents are available only in hard copy, such as video spots about the library program, newspaper articles, and student work. Creating a document file that is arranged in a logical format, such as following the outline on the application form, assists in preparing an index. Often it is easier to create a document index electronically; as items are placed in the file, the index remains current. Later this index may be printed out and placed at the front of the documentation file. Figure 8.3 is an example of a document index that follows the outline on the application form.

NSLMPY Award Index of Documents

Mission Statements
1. District Mission, Goals, Objectives
2. SLMP Mission, Goals, Objectives
3. Evidence that the SLMP and District Mission, Goals, and Objectives Mesh
4. Strategic Plans (District and SLMP)

Implementing the Mission
1. Teacher, Student, Administrator, and Parent Involvement in the Planning Process
2. Evidence that the strategic plan meets local needs
3. Evidence that the SLMP is living its mission

Teaching and Learning
1. Library Media Curriculum
2. Documentation of Collaborative Teaching and Planning
3. Documentation of Collection Depth and Breath
4. Reading Initiatives
5. Instruction Delivery (varied lesson plans and teaching style)
6. Documentation of Student Learning/Achievement
7. Evidence of Student Use (whole class, one-on-one, small group)
8. Information Literacy/Technology benchmarks/assessments
9. Community Involvement

Information Access and Delivery
1. Collection Development Policy & Related Policies
2. Evidence of Physical Access/Building Plan
3. Evidence of Conducive Learning Environment
4. Evidence of Flexible Access
5. District Library Media Policy Manual
6. Evidence of Intellectual Freedom
7. Evidence of Ethical Use of Material

Program Administration
1. District Standards for Teachers & LMS
2. Staffing Standards
3. Management Files (Budget, Orders, Training, Processes)
4. Strategic Plan
5. Evidence of Ongoing Assessment
6. Evidence of Adequate Funding
7. Staff Development Initiatives
8. Professional Development Plan
9. Annual Promotional & Informational Materials

Public Relations
1. Public Relation Plan
2. Evidence of Building Level, Community, and District PR

Figure 8.3. Sample index for supporting documents.

Write a draft description of the program that reflects school and district library policies and procedures and a clear understanding of *Information Power*. Before writing the draft, note the page limitations for each section of the program description. Then create an outline using essential words that describe the key elements of the library media program. Using this outline, write a description for each section of the application. Often it is helpful to ask several members of the school community to read the document to ensure that the information about the program is clearly stated. Each reader provides additional opportunities to refine the quality and content of the document. The library media program description for the NSLMPY award is completed when it explains the extent of

- teacher involvement and collaboration,

- student involvement and learning connections,

- the public relations communication plan,

- joint decision making,

- community involvement, and

- professional growth opportunities.

Although it is tempting to portray a perfect library program, showing how the library media program overcame obstacles lends credence to the application.

Revise and finalize the description of the program to make the document crisp and clear. The assistance of a grammar expert will give the application a professional touch. Often business teachers provide tips on typing and clarify the style of the document. Reworking word choices and sentences by using the *Synonym Finder* by Rodale Press condenses thoughts, targets words, and provides precise descriptors for the document. The program description is finished when it paints a picture of activity in the library and the school generated by a unique school library media program that ensures students and staff are effective users of ideas and information (AASL 2004).

Fill out the AASL application form accurately and completely. This requires a detail-oriented approach. One suggestion is to make working copies of the application form to allow for correction if necessary. When filling out the form, call the AASL office for assistance if some of the sections need clarification. It is wiser to ask for AASL's interpretation than to submit an application that is considered incomplete.

Mail the application packet before the deadline. Late December is a busy mail time, so choose a carrier that ensures delivery by the specified date. The application *cannot be faxed* and must be sent in multiple copies. If using the postal service, paying extra for a return receipt confirms that the material arrived on time. Also, calling the AASL office to verify receipt of the application is acceptable.

Visiting Committee Preparation

Once the library media specialist is notified by AASL that the library media program is a finalist for the award, preparation for the committee's visit is made. Usually, there is not a great deal of time between being notified of the visit and the actual visit. *For this reason, prepare for a visit as soon as the application is sent to AASL.* As soon as the application is mailed, begin preparing for the visit by collecting data, notifying key people, deciding on hospitality, creating a proposed agenda, and continuing to provide daily library instruction.

Collecting data—The crate of documentation that began to accumulate during the application writing process is a starting point for a committee visit. Reviewing the documents and gathering additional evidence that supports the library program are part of an ongoing process. The documents should include a copy of the district mission statement, the school mission statement, and district library policies, such as the consideration of materials. Other district information to include is technology plans, library media program standards of learning, dates and times of district library meetings, and dates and times of library in-services. Building-level sample library lesson plans with evaluation rubrics, flyers for library events, copies of newspaper articles, and printouts of Web articles about the library program all verify the library media program's activities.

Notifying key people—Key library constituents should be available to meet the committee if they are aware of a potential visit. The AASL award committee typically visits between March 1 and April 15. The committee honors the dates on the application that the school indicates are unavailable for the site visit. Knowing this, as soon as the application is mailed, contact the superintendent's office, the school board office, and key parents and ask them to block off time during those six weeks for a possible evaluation committee visit. When contacting the district and community leaders, request any dates when they are unavailable during the visitation window of March 1 thru April 15. Compiling a list of dates when library supporters are available and unavailable gives the library media program supporters the best opportunity to participate in the committee visit.

Deciding on hospitality—Meet with the school hospitality committee chairperson and explain how he or she can help make the day of the visit flow smoothly. The hospitality committee or a group of parents can assist in transporting the committee to and from the school on the day of the visit. They can be in the background providing food and basic amenities, thereby freeing the library media specialist to instruct and carry out a somewhat normal day.

Considering an agenda—Preparing an agenda for a visit provides an outline on who, what, where, when, why, and how the visit will take place. Ask the chair of the awards committee or the AASL's contact what the committee wants on the agenda. The agenda should balance data review, interviews, observations, and question-and-answer time. Figures 8.4 and 8.5 are sample agendas.

AASL Site Visit Agenda for One Day

7:00–7:30 AM	Welcome—the Library Staff School Board Chair SCA—SCA President
7:30–8:00 AM	Meet with School Administrators Principal Assistant Principals
8:30–9:00 AM	Tour of School– Student Representative
9:00–12:00 AM	Observation of Classes Receiving Library Instructions Meet with Students Review Documentation Instructional Specialist of Library Media Services
12:00–12:30 PM	LUNCH
1:00–1:30 PM	Superintendent of Schools
2:00–2:45 PM	Meet with Teachers
3:00–3:30 PM	Meet with Parents
3:30 PM	Return to Hotel
6:00 PM	Dinner/Questions and Answers

Figure 8.4. Sample agenda for one-day site visit.

AASL District Site Visit Agenda for Two Days

Day One	
8:00–9:00 AM	Welcome—the Central Library Staff Video "Library Links"/Continental Breakfast
9:00–9:30 AM	Meet with Superintendents Superintendent of Schools Assistant Superintendent of Instruction
9:45–10:15 AM	Meet with Directors Director, High School Education Director, Middle School Education Director, Elementary School Education
10:15–2:30 PM	Tour of School Libraries (East End) Elementary School, Middle School *(Lunch),* High School
2:30–3:00 PM	Principals' and Teachers' Reception (School Library)
3:00–3:30 PM	Review Documentation/Return to Hotel
6:00 PM	Dinner/Informal Question and Answer Session
Day Two	
8:00–8:30 AM	Continental Breakfast (High School) Meet with Students
9:00–10:00 AM	Review Documentation
10:30–2:20 PM	Tour of School Libraries (West End) Elementary School, Middle School *(Lunch),* High School
2:30–3:00 PM	Parent Reception (School Library)
3:00–3:30 PM	Review Documentation/Questions and Answers/ Return to Hotel
6:00 PM	Dinner/Informal Question and Answer Session

Figure 8.5. Sample agenda for two-day site visit.

Continuing library activities—Once the application packet is sent to AASL, continue with daily library activities. Each week continue to file documentation of lesson plans, evaluation rubrics, weekly calendars, and public relations efforts.

The Review Committee's Visit

Agenda

Prior to the committee's arrival, the chair often indicates what information the committee wants to review and with whom they want to talk. It is critical to provide an agenda that permits the committee to have time to talk with key people and to observe the library media specialist's teaching. When assembling students and staff to talk with the committee, consider providing the committee with passes that they can distribute to any staff member or student they see in the hall. This random method of selecting students and staff conveys an open and confident message about the library program to the committee.

Routine Activities

Providing the committee with the opportunity to observe a routine day requires prior planning because the committee's presence makes the day atypical. An announcement from the principal that introduces the visitors, explains their purpose, and encourages the staff and students to stop by and talk with the committee members conveys confidence and openness. This brief announcement by the principal to staff and students serves to acknowledge the committee and sets the tone for the visit. With the hospitality committee taking care of the committee's comfort needs, and key supporters punctually visiting and conversing with the committee, the library media staff are able to continue providing customary services and instruction.

Unexpected Events

The library media specialist's day often includes the unexpected. Handling the unforeseen is what a library media specialist does well. A visit from committee members who are traveling from all regions of the country is sometimes affected by late flights and traffic delays. It is almost impossible to define and anticipate the unusual situations that might surface.

Should the unexpected occur, brainstorm how to replicate the time and information that the committee is missing. For example, one visiting committee's trip was delayed several hours. If this should happen, videotape the library activities and give the video to the committee. This compensates somewhat for the lost observation time. Library staff should remember that everything does not have to be perfect and that unexpected events are not as important as how these unforeseen situations are handled. Also, a calm response to unforeseen circumstances is an important part of the evaluation.

Endorphin Boost

The entire visitation process creates an endorphin boost for the library media staff, the faculty, and the students. It is the culmination of a focused commitment by the school community to the library media program. Enjoy the validation and the emotional surge created by the NSLMPY award process. Later, take time to reflect on the visit and make notes on what went well and what needs improvement. Then let go of the outcome. The process furnishes the program with unusual opportunities for growth and improvement, thus enhancing student learning in the school. The value is in the doing, not necessarily in the winning. The results of the visit are weeks away, so draw energy from the visit and remember the support from a community that values the library media program.

Concluding Thoughts

Whether or not the library is selected for the award, several important results enhance the library media program. This process identifies community support and validates the library program. The validation comes from the community and the committee. The process stimulates library media program growth because, in attempting to become the best school library media program in the nation, changes occur that bring about improvement and growth. A natural outcome of this process is that new partnerships are built among staff, students, and the community. Perhaps the greatest impact of this award is that it spotlights the library media program's role in the academic achievement of students.

Summary

In this day of high-stakes testing, the assessment of the library media program validates the library–classroom connection. Although the evaluation of the library media program using AASL's rubric with target indicators is ongoing, a thorough assessment is now complete. Documentation data for each goal and objective are available and accessible for review. It is imperative to be organized when applying for the NSLMPY award. Developing a time line that targets completion dates for each component of the NSLMPY award application makes the submission process less overwhelming. The ten-step application process includes obtaining an application form; reviewing and clarifying the award criteria and rules; creating a time line; collecting data; eliciting staff, student, and community input; organizing the documentation; writing a draft description of the program; revising and finalizing the description of the program; filling out the AASL application form; and mailing the application packet before the deadline. Usually, there is not a great deal of time between being notified of the committee's visit and the actual visit. *For this reason, prepare for a visit as soon as the application is sent to AASL* by collecting data, notifying key people, deciding on hospitality, creating a proposed agenda, and continuing to provide daily library instruction. Whether or not the library is selected for the award, the greatest impact is that it spotlights the library media program's role in the academic achievement of students.

Resources

American Association of School Librarians (AASL). 2004. *National School Library Media Program of the Year award application.* Chicago. Available at: http://www.ala.org/ala/aasl/aaslawards/ natlslmprogram/ 2005nslmpyapp.pdf (accessed November 11, 2004).

Appendix A
American Association of
School Librarians Documents

Learning and Teaching Principles of School Library Media Programs*

Principle 1:   The library media program is essential to learning and teaching and must be fully integrated into the curriculum to promote students' achievement of learning goals.

Principle 2:   The information literacy standards for student learning are integral to the content and objectives of the school's curriculum.

Principle 3:   The library media program models and promotes collaborative planning and curriculum development.

Principle 4:   The library media program models and promotes creative, effective, and collaborative teaching.

Principle 5:   Access to the full range of information resources and services through the library media program is fundamental to learning.

Principle 6:   The library media program encourages and engages students in reading, viewing, and listening for understanding and enjoyment.

Principle 7:   The library media program supports the learning of all students and other members of the learning community who have diverse learning abilities, styles, and needs.

Principle 8:   The library media program fosters individual and collaborative inquiry.

Principle 9:   The library media program integrates the uses of technology for learning and teaching.

Principle 10:   The library media program is an essential link to the larger learning community.

These principles were identified and developed by the Information Power Vision Committee, reviewed and commented upon by the profession, and approved by the AASL and AECT Boards as the cardinal premises on which learning and teaching within the effective school library media program is based.

*From Information Power: Building Partnerships for Learning by the American Association of School Librarians and Association for Educational Communications and Technology. Copyright 1998 by the American Association of School Librarians and Association for Educational Communications and Technology. Reprinted by permission of the American Library Association.

Information Access and Delivery Principles of School Library Media Programs**

Principle 1:   The library media program provides intellectual access to information and ideas for learning.

Principle 2:   The library media program provides physical access to information and resources for learning.

Principle 3:   The library media program provides a climate that is conducive to learning.

Principle 4:   The library media program requires flexible and equitable access to information, ideas, and resources for learning.

Principle 5:   The collections of the library media program are developed and evaluated collaboratively to support the school's curriculum and to meet the diverse learning needs of students.

Principle 6:   The library media program is founded on a commitment to the right of intellectual freedom.

Principle 7:   The library media program policies, procedures, and practices of the library media program reflect legal guidelines and professional ethics.

These principles were identified and developed by the Information Power Vision Committee, reviewed and commented upon by the profession, and approved by the AASL and AECT Boards as the cardinal premises on which learning and teaching within the effective school library media program is based.

Program Administration Principles of School Library Media Programs***

Principle 1:   The library media program supports the mission, goals, objectives, and continuous improvement of the school.

Principle 2:   In every school, a minimum of one full-time, certified/licensed library media specialist supported by qualified staff is fundamental to the implementation of an effective library media program at the building level.

Principle 3:   An effective library media program requires a level of professional and support staffing that is based upon a school's instructional programs, services, facilities, size, and numbers of students and teachers.

Principle 4:   An effective library media program requires ongoing administrative support.

Principle 5:   Comprehensive and collaborative long-range, strategic planning is essential to the effectiveness of the library media program.

Principle 6:   Ongoing assessment for improvement is essential to the vitality of an effective library media program.

Principle 7:   Sufficient funding is fundamental to the success of the library media program.

Principle 8:   Ongoing staff development—both to maintain professional knowledge and skills and to provide instruction in information literacy for teachers, administrators, and other members of the learning community—is an essential component of the library media program.

Principle 9:   Clear communication of the mission, goals, functions and impact of the library media program is necessary to the effectiveness of the program.

Principle 10:   Effective management of human, financial, and physical resources undergirds a strong library media program.

These principles were identified and developed by the Information Power Vision Committee, reviewed and commented upon by the profession, and approved by the AASL and AECT Boards as the cardinal premises on which learning and teaching within the effective school library media program is based.

Appendix B
Forms and Techniques

Chesterfield County Acceptable Use Policy*

School Board Policy 723 Acceptable Use - the CCPS-NET

The responsible use of computers and computer networks is a powerful tool in the support of the instructional program. Regulation 723.1 outlines acceptable and unacceptable use of the CCPS-NET, a wide area network linking the schools, administrative offices, and the Internet.

Regulation 723.1

Vision

In support of the Chesterfield County Public Schools mission, access to the CCPS-NET will:

- provide connections to world wide resources, and;
- facilitate local, regional, and world wide communications.

Acceptable Use

- The CCPS-NET is established solely for educational purposes.
- The CCPS-NET is a shared resource and will only fulfill its mission when used appropriately.
- CCPS-NET account owners are responsible for all activities under their account.
- Any CCPS-NET user's traffic that traverses another network may be subject to that network's acceptable use policy.
- Photographs of students may be included in World Wide Web documents provided no personal information is included.

Unacceptable Use

- Any use of the CCPS-NET for commercial purposes or political lobbying is prohibited.

*Reprinted by permission of Chesterfield County Public Schools.

- Any use of the CCPS-NET for illegal, inappropriate, or obscene purposes, or in support of such activities, is prohibited. Illegal activities shall be defined as a violation of local, state, or federal laws. Inappropriate use shall be defined a s a violation of the intended use of the network, including the intentional introduction of viruses, corruption of systems, files and resources.

- Any use of the CCPS-NET for purposes in conflict with approved School Board policies & procedures is prohibited. School Board Policy 720 prohibits the illegal copying of documents, software, and other materials.

- Great care shall be taken by the CCPS-NET administrators to ensure the right of privacy of users; however, all students, educators and parents have the responsibility to take appropriate action when becoming aware of unacceptable usage.

Use of Networked Resources

- Network Accessible Resources (NAR's) must be used in support of the instructional program.

- Exploration of NAR's is to be conducted within the context of supporting the instructional program, and should be performed with a defined purpose or goal.

- NAR's will not be used as the sole research source, but rather will be considered with all research tools available in the library and/or classroom.

- Given the fluid nature of many NAR's, students and staff must evaluate the validity and appropriateness of use of a particular resource for a given assignment or application.

CCPS-NET Access & Accounts

- Access to the CCPS-NET is considered a privilege and is permitted to the extent that available resources allow.

- All Chesterfield County Public School personnel and retirees are eligible for a CCPS-NET account on the CCPS-NET server.

- Students in grades K-5 will have access to the CCPS-NET through a classroom account managed by school personnel.

- Students in grades 6-12 will have access to the CCPS-NET through a classroom account managed by school personnel, and may be granted an individual account held jointly by the student and parent/guardian.

- Community members are encouraged to access the CCPS-NET through third party Internet providers.

- From time to time, the Chesterfield County Schools will make decisions on whether specific uses of the CCPS-NET are consistent with this policy. The Chesterfield County Schools shall remain the final authority on use of the network and the issuance and cancellation of user accounts.

World Wide Web Access—Unfiltered Accounts

The Chesterfield County Schools provide access to the World Wide Web (WWW) via the CCPS-NET. Standard use of the WWW utilizes a proxy server based filter that screens for non-curriculum related pages. Due to the nature of such filtering technology, the filter may at times filter pages that are appropriate for staff & student research. To facilitate the access of appropriate pages that the filter blocks, unfiltered accounts may be granted that bypass the filter.

Unfiltered accounts will be granted to any staff member who states, in writing, that they need such an account to facilitate the programs of the Chesterfield Schools. *Such accounts will never be granted to students.* Staff should be aware that all web access by such unfiltered accounts is logged by the server and that these logs may be reviewed by the system administrators periodically during normal system maintenance.

Electronic Mail

Electronic mail (email) is provided to staff and secondary students in support of the instructional program and its support services. Acceptable use of email is based on common sense, common decency and civility as applied to all communications wit hin the electronic environment.

In addition to the broad acceptable use principals outlined in Regulation 723.1, and the conduct issues outlined in Regulation 401.1, the following unacceptable uses of email are specifically delineated:

- Sending harassing, abusive, or offensive material to or about others
- Intercepting, altering, or disrupting electronic mail systems and/or messages
- Introducing messages to email systems with the intent to cause network congestion

Electronic communications are protected by the same laws and policies, and are subject to the same limitations as other types of media. When using or storing messages on the network, the user should consider both the personal ramifications and the impa ct on the school system should the messages be disclosed or released to other parties. Extreme caution should be used when committing confidential information to the network as its confidentiality cannot be guaranteed. Messages sent to the wrong address could be used inappropriately and the receiver could save the information indefinitely. From time to time, the administrators of the email system may review email logs and or messages as a part of the standard maintenance and security schedule. ***Employees and students should not consider email as private.***

Collaborative Teaching Evaluation Form

Teacher _____ Project Title _____

Total library time for project _____ Number of students involved _____

Explain with examples what the easiest part of the research project was.

Explain with examples what the most difficult part of the research project was.

What resources were most helpful for this project?

Were the information literacy skills taught effective for this project?

What should be done differently if this project is repeated?

Did the project benefit from collaboration? _____ yes _____ no
If yes, explain how.

Were the library resources useful for the project? Rate them using the following scale.

Scale:

5 = excellent 4 = above average 3 = average 2 = below average 1 = inadequate

_____ print

_____ electronic databases

_____ Internet

Additional comments:

James River High School Computer Code of Ethics Agreement

I, _____, a student at James River High School agree to the following Computer Code of Ethics:

- I understand that the James River High School network belongs to James River High School and is designed for educational purposes.

- I understand that my access to this network or any computers at James River High School is a privilege, not a right.

- I will use the computer hardware and software for authorized educational purposes only and will not enter the DOS or Novell operating systems OR any file server on which I do not have a valid user ID of my own.

- I understand that I will be held responsible for any damage I cause to computer hardware and software while I am a student at James River High School.

- I understand that no software of any form (including, but not limited to applications and viruses) is to be loaded onto any part of the network or onto any computer at James River High School.

- I understand that no hardware, software, software documentation, or diskette is to be removed from its specific location on the network or in the school.

- I will not share any of my passwords nor will I use anyone else's password to access their account.

- I understand that no individual has any rights to copy, modify, or access another individual's files.

- I understand that I am responsible for logging off the network after completing my work.

- I will not give or receive any unauthorized assistance relating to hardware, software, or computer class work.

- I will report any hardware or software malfunction to the supervising teacher immediately AND BEFORE rebooting the computer.

- I understand that appropriate classroom behavior is expected at all times near any computer or in any computer lab and that I am responsible for cleaning my work area at the end of the period.

- I will abide by the rule that no food or drink is permitted near any computers or in any computer labs.

- I understand that any violation of this Code of Ethics will result in disciplinary action as determined by the supervising teacher, Network Administrator, and/or the Administration. This could include, and is not limited to, the suspension of computer access privileges.

Student Signature: _____**Date:** _____

Parent/Guardian Signature: _____

Library Memo—Goals and Objectives

DATE: 09/15/2003

TO: PRINCIPAL

FROM: LIBRARY MEDIA SPECIALISTS

RE: 2003-2004 LIBRARY DEPARTMENT GOALS

Teaching and Learning

1. Provide target literacy standards integration training for departments. The training will highlight projects that can be completed in 20-minute blocks of time.

2. Instruct students and staff on new databases highlighting the product changes.

3. Focus student instruction on the importance and difference of three specific sources of information: print, paid databases, Internet.

Information Access and Delivery

1. Facilitate participation in the metropolitan area reading program with special focus on the school community's participation..

2. Pursue alternate sources of funding (i.e., grants, awards) to facilitate the purchase of new technologies.

3. Continue to develop special programs to create library awareness and reach out to varying student interests and curriculum areas.

4. Develop plans for literature circles and book chats.

Program Administration

1. Develop an "adopt-a-shelf" program to foster student library responsibility and encourage efficient daily operation of the library.

2. Provide a "student forum" for input and assessment of the library media program.

3. Participate on curriculum and technology committees on the building, county and state level.

4. Continue active involvement in state professional organizations.

Joint Planning Form (Elementary)

Teacher's Name: _____ Date of Activity: _____

Class Size: _____ Standard of Learning: _____

Classroom Activities (prior to library media center visit):

Lesson Objectives:

Library Media Center Activities:

Print, Electronic, and Internet Resources:

Materials Needed:

Evaluation of Activity:

James River High School
LIBRARY MEDIA CENTER
Joint Planning Form

TEACHER: _____

CLASS PERIOD: _____

GRADE/LEVEL: _____

LIBRARY DATE(S): _____

CONTENT
AREA:_____

RELATED
S.O.L.('S):_____

CLASS SIZE:

_____

Classroom Teacher's Responsibility	Library Media Specialist's Responsibility

Electronic Resources

DISCovering Authors _____

Granger's World of Poetry _____

Exploring Poetry _____

Exploring Shakespeare _____

Shelf for the Masterplots Complete _____

Exploring Novels _____

Exploring Short Stories _____

SIRs Researcher Online as at least SIRS
   Government Reporter Online _____

SIRS Renaissance Online _____

U*X*L* Biographies _____

DISCovering Biography_____

Description:

   Magill's Survey of Science _____

   DISCovering Science _____

   DISCovering Nations, States,
     and Cultures _____

   American Decades _____

   DISCovering U.S. History _____

   DISCovering World History _____

   World Book Infofinder _____

   Grolier Online _____

   GaleNet _____

   Other Internet Resources _____

Suggested Web Site _____

Suggested Print Resources

Books Placed on Overnight Reserve

following dates:

May students use the Encyclopedia as one resource?

Evaluation of student Learning Completed Project

Date Due:

Bibliography Required?

ABILITIES, INTERESTS, AND SPECIAL NEEDS OF STUDENTS:

Please Attach a Copy of the Student Assignment

WEEK OF:

PERIOD	MONDAY	TUESDAY	WEDNESDAY	THURSDAY	FRIDAY
1					
2/3					
4/5 1st Lunch					
4/5 2nd Lunch					
4/5 3rd Lunch					
4/5 4th Lunch					
6/7					

Weekly Calendar

Library Media Program Survey

The library media staff is in the process of reviewing the current library media services offered in our school. Please help us in our decision making by indicating the importance of these services to you as they relate to the educational needs of our students. We appreciate your comments as a way to better understand your responses to the questions.

RESPONSE SCALE

1. **Not very much**   **(to a small degree)**
2. **Moderately**   **(quarterly)**
3. **Frequently**   **(monthly)**
4. **Extremely**   **(to a very high degree)**

1. To what degree do you use library materials or services?

     1   2   3   4

     Please give additional information to clarify your response.

     _____

     _____

2. To what degree is the technology available in the library media center "user friendly?"

     1   2   3   4

     Please give additional information to clarify your response.

     _____

     _____

3. To what degree are the library skills (information literacy skills) effectively integrated with your class assignments?

     1   2   3   4

     Please give additional information to clarify your response.

     _____

     _____

4. To what degree are resource materials available to support your class assignments?

     1   2   3   4

     Please give additional information to clarify your response.

     _____

     _____

RESPONSE SCALE

1.	Not very much	(to a small degree)
2.	Moderately	(quarterly)
3.	Frequently	(monthly)
4.	Extremely	(to a very high degree)

5. To what degree are requests for assistance met in a timely manner?

   1   2   3   4

   Please give additional information to clarify your response.

   _____

   _____

6. To what degree is the library media staff helpful?

   1   2   3   4

   Please give additional information to clarify your response.

   _____

   _____

7. The three things I like best about the library are:

   _____

   _____

   _____

8. How has the library helped you the most this year?

   _____

   _____

9. What changes would you like to make in the library program, if any, and why?

   _____

   _____

10. Would you like the library to continue the extended hours on Wednesday next year? _____yes _____no

Thank you for taking the time to complete this survey. Your input will be considered in our future plans.

Needs Analysis Survey

Name (optional): _____ Date: _____

Please take a few minutes to answer these questions carefully and candidly. The purpose of this survey is to determine whether the library media program meets your needs. Your comments will help identify areas of the library media program that can be improved.

Strongly Agree = SA   Agree = A   Neutral = N
Disagree = D   Strongly Disagree = SD

Learning and Teaching

1. Student library skills are integrated into class assignments.   SA   A   N   D   SD
2. The librarian collaborates instructionally with teachers.   SA   A   N   D   SD
3. The librarian is involved in curriculum planning.   SA   A   N   D   SD
4. The librarian's teaching methods are varied and effective.   SA   A   N   D   SD
5. Reading for enrichment and pleasure is encouraged.   SA   A   N   D   SD
6. Students' varied learning styles are well supported.   SA   A   N   D   SD
7. Students develop individual search strategies.   SA   A   N   D   SD
8. Student learning is assessed.   SA   A   N   D   SD

Information Access and Delivery

1. The library accommodates multiple classes.   SA   A   N   D   SD
2. Library print and electronic resources meet my needs.   SA   A   N   D   SD
3. The library environment encourages student use.   SA   A   N   D   SD
4. Access to library resources meets my needs.   SA   A   N   D   SD
5. The library resources are well-balanced in all formats.   SA   A   N   D   SD
6. The principles of intellectual freedom are supported.   SA   A   N   D   SD
7. Ethical issues such as copyright and fair use are implemented.   SA   A   N   D   SD

Program Administration

1. The library staffing is sufficient to meet user needs.   SA   A   N   D   SD
2. The library staff communicates with department heads regularly.   SA   A   N   D   SD
3. Useful professional development workshops are provided.   SA   A   N   D   SD
4. Library materials are accessible and easy to find.   SA   A   N   D   SD

Your answers to these questions will help us improve services. THANKS!

1. How has the library helped you most this year?

2. What, if anything, would you change about the library program?

3. List professional development needs that you would like the library staff to address.

Needs Analysis Tabulation Form

Need	SA	A	N	D	SD
LT - Student library skills are integrated into class assignments.					
LT - The librarian collaborates instructionally with teachers.					
LT - The librarian is involved in curriculum planning.					
LT - The librarian's teaching methods are varied and effective.					
LT - Reading for enrichment and pleasure is encouraged.					
LT - Students' varied learning styles are well supported.					
LT - Students develop individual search strategies.					
LT - Student learning is assessed.					
LT - Other					
LT - Other					
LT - Other					
IAD - The library accommodates multiple classes.					
IAD - Library print and electronic resources meet my needs.					
IAD - The library environment encourages student use.					
IAD - Access to library resources meets my needs.					
IAD - The library resources are well-balanced in all formats.					
IAD - The principles of intellectual freedom are supported.					
IAD - Ethical issues such as copyright and fair use are implemented.					
IAD - Other					
IAD - Other					
IAD - Other					
PA - The library staffing is sufficient to meet user needs.					
PA - The library staff communicates with department heads regularly.					
PA - Useful professional development workshops are provided.					
PA - Library materials are accessible and easy to find.					
PA - Other					
PA - Other					
PA - Other					

LT =   Learning and Teaching
IAD = Information Access Delivery
PA =   Program Administration

Sample Agenda

Library Program Improvement Team Meeting
3/15/2004

2:00–2:15   Team member introductions and welcome

2:15–2:30   Review of project mission, goals, objectives

2:30–2:45   Team meeting ground rules

2:45–2:55   Team members create individual lists by responding to the following question.

- What do you consider to be the most important aspect of the library media program?

2:55–3:10   Team members review, discuss, and reach consensus on top three or four components of the library media program.

3:10–3:15   Comparison of core team priorities to the team priorities

3:15–3:20   Homework

- compare the list of priorities to the library media program vision and mission

- compare the library media program vision and mission to the school vision and mission

- e-mail discrepancies between the priorities to the team for discussion

3:20–3:30   Questions?

Next meeting: 3/22/2004, 2:00 p.m., library conference room

Sample Form/Team Meeting Minutes

Library Program Improvement Team Meeting Minutes
(Date)

Members present:

1.   Discussion Point:

        DECIDED OUTCOME:

2.   Discussion Point:

        DECIDED OUTCOME:

3.   Discussion Point:

        DECIDED OUTCOME:

4.   Discussion Point:

        DECIDED OUTCOME:

Assignments for next meeting:

Next meeting date:

Sample Lesson Plans

Ancient River Civilizations

Objectives: The students will:

1.   locate information using a variety of formats with special emphasis on print materials and specialized databases.

2.   select information appropriate to the curriculum assignment.

3.   conduct Internet searches in accordance with the district Acceptable Use Policy.

4.   participate in determining information needs of the group.

Activities:

1.   Review login procedures.

2.   Identify print materials specific to this assignment.

3.   Use data projector to identify electronic resources for this assignment.

4.   Discuss key word strategies.

5.   Identify Internet access through search engines.

6.   Individual research.

7.   Teacher and librarians will assist students as needed.

Evaluation: Student notes and information. Student project.

Public Policy

Objectives: The students will:

1. refine strategies for selecting appropriate sources for research and recreational reading.

2. distinguish between fact, opinion, point of view and propaganda.

3. select information appropriate to the curriculum assignment.

4. collaborate with others to design, develop, and evaluate information products and solutions.

5. communicate ideas in presenting a group project.

Activities:

1. Identify a need—relate to school experience, ex. parking passes.

2. Identify print sources of information:
   Current topics series. (Taking Sides, Opposing Viewpoints, Current Controversies, Contemporary World Issues, Editorials on file)

   Almanac

3. Identify electronic sources of information:
   ProQuest Direct
   SIRS
   GaleNet

4. Discuss keyword strategies.

5. Discuss evaluation of web sites: authority, accuracy, objectivity, coverage and currency.

Evaluation: Observation of research and review completed projects based on rubric.

World Language Research

Objectives: The students will:

1. refine search strategies for print and electronic sources related to the curriculum assignment.

2. locate information using a variety of formats with special emphasis on print materials and specialized databases.

3. evaluate accuracy, relevance, and comprehensiveness of information as it relates to the curriculum assignment.

4. prepare a five minute presentation on his or her topic.

Activities:

1. Identify sources of information:
    A.   Larousse Encyclopedias
    B.   French Dictionaries
    C.   Current Biography (indexed on ProQuest Direct)
    D.   UXL Biographies
    E.   Subject specific sources—<u>Contemporary Musicians</u>.
    F.   GaleNet

2. Review search paths to sources.

3. Teacher and Librarians will assist as needed.

Evaluation: Student research strategies, note taking, and final presentation.

Schoolwide Team Fact Sheet

Evaluation of the Library Media Program

Mission: The school community will assist the library media staff to facilitate the merging of the library users' needs with the principles outlined in *Information Power*. The outcome will be a library media program that is exemplary and worthy of the NSLMPY award.

Goals:

The school community committee will assist the library staff:

- A. Evaluate the status of the current library media program.
- B. Develop and implement a needs analysis.
- C. Compare the current library media program to target indicators in *Information Power*.
- D. Develop an action plan based on results from the needs analysis and the principles of *Information Power*.
- E. Create a model library media program.

Time Line:

February 1st	Library staff reads *Information Power*
February 15th	Library staff identifies library program priorities
February 22nd	Library staff compares priorities to existing vision and mission
March 1st	Library staff identifies school-wide team members
March 8th	Library staff provides background information to school-wide team
March 15th	School-wide team meets to identify library priorities
March 22nd	School-wide team clarifies questionnaire
March 29th	Questionnaire is distributed to school staff
April 10th	Results from questionnaire are tabulated
April 20th	Needs analysis is conducted
May 1st	Needs are compared to criteria from the *Information Power* rubric
May 10th	An action plan is developed
June	Three program priorities are identified to implement

Search Strategy

Search Strategy

Research topic: _____

Possible Sources of Information:

_____

_____

_____

_____

_____

_____

_____

_____

_____

_____

_____

_____

Keywords: **Related Topics:**

_____   _____

_____   _____

_____   _____

_____   _____

_____   _____

Appendix C
Workshop Plans

Destination Activity

Mission: To illustrate the importance of collaboration for academic achievement.

Goal: Participants will understand the concept that teamwork and collaboration positively affect the outcome of an assignment, project, or goal.

Objective: Teachers and library media specialists will work together on a realistic but fun puzzle that is completed through teamwork.

Time: This activity will take approximately 15 minutes.

Materials:

1. Sets of destination puzzles for each participant

2. Envelopes for the puzzle pieces

3. Basic directions on a sheet of paper

4. Map of local area

5. Markers (different colors for each group)

Activity:

1. Introduce objectives for the activity.

2. Provide each participant with five simple but mixed-up street directions to a familiar local spot. (Do not identify the starting point or ending point.)

3. Ask the participants to determine the destination.

4. After five minutes place the participants into groups with directions to find the ending location.

5. Continue to enlarge the group until the destination point is determined.

6. Have each group map the ending location.

7. Share the answers.

Note: Businesses will often provide coupons or gift certificates that may be handed out to the group that solves the puzzle.

Needs Analysis Workshop

Mission: To conduct a needs analysis that provides the library media specialist with a synthesis of its users' needs.

Goal: Library users will provide information that serves as a basis for developing an action plan that incorporates library users' needs with the library media program's components of learning and teaching, information access and delivery, and program administration.

Objectives:

1.   The participants will express their library needs in a pictorial format.

2.   The needs of the participants will be organized into the categories (a) learning and teaching, (b) information access and delivery, and (c) program administration.

3.   The user needs will be prioritized.

Time: This workshop will take approximately one and one-half hours.

Materials:

1.   4 different types of candy, 20 total pieces of candy

2.   5 pieces of butcher paper

3.   5 packs of magic markers

4.   Flip chart and markers

5.   Masking tape

6.   Different colored stickers (60 blue, 60 red)

Activities:

1.   Introduce objectives for the workshop.

2.   Hand out the candy randomly to divide participants into five groups of four. Participants with the same type of candy form a group.

3.   Give each group the following instructions:

   a.   Without using any words or numbers, draw a picture of the ideal library.

   b.   Be able to explain your representation.

4.   Set a time limit of about 20 minutes for each group to discuss and draw their picture.

5. Gather the groups together, and one by one have each group explain their picture. Each library characteristic described is an expressed need. List these needs under one of the three categories: (a) learning and teaching, (b) information access and delivery, and (c) program administration.

6. Once all groups have explained their pictures, ask the groups to reconvene and discuss their top two priorities for each area: (a) learning and teaching, (b) information access and delivery, and (c) program administration.*

7. Set a time limit of about 15 minutes.*

8. Give each member of the workshop three blue and three red stickers. Each person will go to the flip chart pages taped to the wall and place a blue sticker next to his or her number one priority and a red sticker next to his or her number two priority in each category: (a) learning and teaching, (b) information access and delivery, and (c) program administration.

9. Together all the workshop participants review the needs that have the largest total number of blue stickers.

10. Together all the workshop participants review the needs that have the largest total number of red stickers.

11. Count the stickers beside each need, and on a flip chart write the three top priorities for each category, (a) learning and teaching, (b) information access and delivery, and (c) program administration, based on the placement of the stickers.

Repeat this workshop with as many groups as needed. Use with all staff and a representative group of students. Tabulate the results to determine the three top priorities under each of the three principle categories of *Information Power*.

* If time is short these steps may be eliminated.

Bibliography

American Association of School Librarians (AASL). *AASL Publications and Journals: Information Power Books & Products.* 2004. Available at: http://www.ala.org/ala/aasl/aaslpubsandjournals/ informationpowerbook/informationpowerbooks.htm (accessed July 5, 2004).

―――. *National School Library Media Program of the Year Award Application.* Chicago, 2004. Available at: http://www.ala.org/ ala/aasl/aaslawards/natlslmprogram/2005nslmpyapp.pdf (accessed November 14, 2004).

―――. *A Planning Guide for Information Power: Building Partnerships for Learning with School Library Media Program Assessment Rubric for the 21st Century.* Chicago: American Association of School Librarians/American Library Association, 1999.

American Library Association (ALA). *Position Statement on the Role of the Library Media Specialist in Outcomes-Based Education.* Chicago, 1994. Available at: http://www.ala.org/ala/aasl/ aaslproftools/positionstatements/aaslpositionstatementrolelibrar y.htm (accessed September 20, 2004).

American Library Association (ALA) and the Association for Educational Communications and Technology (AECT). *Information Power: Building Partnerships for Learning.* Chicago: American Library Association and the Association for Educational Communications, 1998.

Dobson, James. *The New Dare to Discipline.* Wheaton, IL: Tyndale House Publishers, 1992.

Fullan, Michael. *The New Meaning of Educational Change.* 3rd ed. New York: Teachers College Press, 2001.

―――. "The Three Stories of Education Reform." *Phi Delta Kappan* (April 2000). Available at: http://web7.infotrac.galenet.com/itw/ infomark/280/10/61585257w7/purl=rc1_EAIM_0_A61557299 &dyn=15!xrn_2_0_A61557299?sw_aep=midl84745 (accessed March 25, 2005).

Hartzell, Gary. *Building Influence for the School Librarian: Tenets, Targets, & Tactics.* 2nd ed. Worthington, OH: Linworth Publishing, 2003.

Lance, Keith Curry, and David V. Loertscher. *Powering Achievement: School Library Media Programs Make a Difference: The Evidence Mounts.* 2nd ed. San Jose, CA: Hi Willow Research & Publishing, 2002.

Senge, Peter. "Building Learning Organizations." *Journal for Quality and Participation* (March 1992): 30–39.

Shashkin, Marshall, and Kenneth J. Kiser. *Putting Total Quality Management to Work: What TQM Means, How to Use It and How to Sustain It over the Long Run.* San Francisco: Berrett-Koehler Publishers, 1993.

Titus, John, Letter to American Association of School Librarians, January 17, 2002.

———. Letter to American Association of School Librarians, January 28, 2003.

Index

About the Author

ANN M. MARTIN is currently serving as Educational Specialist for Library Information Services for the Henrico County Public Schools, Richmond, Virginia. Her former school, the James River High School in Chesterfield, Virginia, is the 2002 recipient of the AASL National School Library Media Program of the Year Award. She has 25 years' experience as a library media specialist.